Work The Future! Today

Finding your path to purpose, passion and profit

Three steps to *unleashing* your potential.
By Whitney Vosburgh + Charlie Grantham

WORK THE FUTURE! TODAY INTRODUCES
THE ART OF THE POSSIBLE, PRACTICED WELL IN ADVANCE.

This is Version 1 of this book,
which is the first **WTF!** book in a series
on Working The Future! Today.

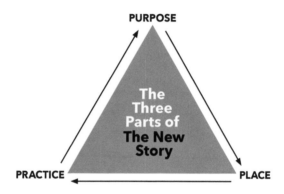

www.workthefuture.today

A **WTF!** Book, V. 1

ISBN-13: 978-0-9996346-0-8

DEDICATION

To **Barry Tuchfeld** ~
friend, mensch, visionary,
and without whom this
book would not exist.

"Work The Future! Today is an ebullient paean to the power of story. What we need, the authors preach, is a new story based on purpose, not on profit. With a mind toward sustaining the planet rather than just amassing money, this book guides you to finding and aligning your purpose, passion, and goals to create that new life-embracing story for yourself, your organization, and the world."

~Daniel H. Pink, Author of DRIVE

TESTIMONIALS

"This is an amazing book—I'll watch for Charlie and Whitney on Good Morning America since this is going to catch on fire. This book offers the next chapter for aligning purpose and life goals in a new and visionary way. Finally, a way to articulate why all the material success often feels empty. This book hits its stride for many of us searching alignment of core beliefs with the "what's next" discussion."
~ **Sharon Klun**, former Manager, Work/Life/Wellness Initiatives, Accenture, and Global Work/Life Initiatives, American Express

"Work The Future! Today captures the essence of the evolutionary shift underway in business from a limited purpose of maximizing profit for shareholders to a broader purpose of creating public benefit. This book explains why the purpose driven business movement as expressed by Benefit Corporations, Certified B Corporations and the Conscious Capitalism movement is so compelling and powerful."
~ **John Montgomery**, Founder of Lex Ultima, and Author of *Great From the Start: How Conscious Corporations Attract Success*

"With their call to action for a better future, Whitney and Charlie articulate a critical need in these chaotic times, and offer a clear path to achieving it—they draw on what's clearly a wealth of experience. The result is a map to the future: a way to ensure we all know what we need to do to thrive."
~ **Ceil Tilney**, former General Manager, Imperative

1

TESTIMONIALS

"*Work The Future! Today is an attention getting book* that travels across our current state of seismic transition through timeless questions and the latest tools of analysis. A world that feels like it has lost its purpose is a world caught in the chasm of this seismic shift. Grantham and Vosburgh begin with personal grounding and build outward to collective renewal. I enjoy the deeply provocative questions they raise and the accessible writing and road map they provide."
~ **Rex Miller**, Futurist and Principal for mindSHIFT, and Co-author of *Change Your Space: How Engaging Workplaces Lead to Transformation and Growth*

"*WTF! is a primer in the value of practicing old wisdom in a new world.* The built environment exists, by definition, outside ourselves. But if you're engaged in transforming it—particularly the spaces and places where people live, work, and play—the authors show that if you want to be effective, you must start by renewing what's within. "
~ **Natalie Grasso**, Editor, *Work Design Magazine*

"*As always, Charlie and Whitney are one step ahead.* I can still remember learning the old "four-Ps" of marketing and they stuck with me. But in hindsight, that model has a huge hole in it: purpose. It is today's currency."
~ **Ryan Johnson**, Executive Director, Executive and Professional Education, ASU Global Institute of Sustainability

2

TESTIMONIALS

"It's in these times of great transition, that true leaders emerge. Work The Future! Today offers comprehensive insights into how we got here, how we can all step up, and what to do next... to make real, positive change happen. More than a clarion call, this book offers a wealth of perspectives and actionable inspiration that's much needed in the chaos/opportunity of the early 21st century. I invite every entrepreneur, leader, and visionary to read this book so we can all make positive change happen."
~ **Ben Gioia**, #1 Best Selling Author of *Influence With A Heart*

"The book looks really wonderful! Many of the issues that my coalition, Napa Vision 2050, has dealt with in organizing and moving forward to involve citizens in our future, particularly community fabric and watersheds—are covered in the book. There is so much about community building now, and that makes me hopeful, even in this very dark period."
~ **Patricia Damery**, Community Organizer, Jungian Analyst, and Author of *Farming Soul: A Tale of Initiation*

"If you want to improve and stay ahead of the curve without losing your soul, this is the book! Charlie and Whitney expand beyond Simon Sinek's "Start with Why" and argue convincingly that place should have a purpose, too."
~ **Rebecca Ryan**, Author of *Regeneration: A Manifesto for America's Next Leaders*

3

TESTIMONIALS

"We are moving into a new period that require new stories and new symbols. Charles Grantham, and his co-author Whitney Vosburgh, are the best guides and coaches for those who want to take advantage of this new period. Highly recommended."
~ **John Fraim**, Author of *Battle of Symbols*

"Whitney and Charlie have crystallized how much Purpose is the driving force behind the passion I was able to generate with my community engagement work. Align your company with people's higher purpose and deep engagement will follow."
~ **Mark Finnern**, Founder of Playful Enterprise, and former Chief Community Evangelist, SAP

"WTF! describes how crossing the chasm between old and new is going to require people to get clear on personal purpose, and links that to the purposes of their workplace and larger social community."
~ **Gabriella Lettini**, Ph.D., Dean of the Faculty of Starr King School for the Ministry, Graduate Theological Union, and Author of *Soul Repair: Recovering from Moral Injury After War*

TESTIMONIALS

"*Work The Future! Today presents an inspiring alternative to the typical workplace where too often it is like going to jail and with similarly unproductive results. Vosburgh and Grantham show how to transform the workplace so that it embodies the shared purpose of all its stakeholders. Follow their refreshing approach and everything changes for the better—productivity, work place satisfaction, and, yes, even profitability.*"
~ **Ralph "Jake" Warner**, Co-founder and former Executive Chairman of Nolo Press, pioneer of the self-help law movement, and author of many books including "Retire Happy"

"*Looks like the perfect follow up on my "Thrivability: Breaking through to a World that Works" book. Congratulations. I love it.*"
~ **Jean Russell**, Co-Founder of Thrivable Futures Inc., and Author of *Thrivability: Breaking through to a World that Works*

"*Work The Future! Today shows leaders how to co-create communities where people want to be. Whitney and Charlie cut a new path to help leaders see blind spots and where old thinking limits their community's potential.*"
~ **Trina Hoefling**, Author of *Working Virtually: Transforming the Mobile Workplace*, and Co-founder, The SMART Workplace and Virtual Workplace University

TESTIMONIALS

"WTF! is happening now! The fight is on for those of us who daily Work The Future! Today within impoverished communities surrounded by an abundance of natural and human resources. Like the prophets of ancient civilizations, whose influence continues to be felt in "modern" civilization, Whitney and Charlie are calling out to our peoples, our new world of local and international neighbors, awakening our hearts and minds to receive new, resurrected ancient truth; sounding the alarm— sharing the vision—the plan for our escape to attain truth, liberty, justice for our people, our planet, our prosperity. They offer everyone within these pages the lifeline many of us carry forth daily onto our community recovery battlefields. Take heart, have faith, take action and join us in restoring purpose, place, practice."
~ **MelanieFae Garrett**, Valley Fire Disaster Recovery Manager, American Red Cross, and Community Restoration Advocate, No Boundaries

"This is really exciting. Understanding a clear sense of purpose and place, and knowing the story you are living and telling is so important and sadly lacking in many organizations."
~ **Jon Braslaw**, Director, Business Process Improvement, Recology

"Work The Future! Today is extraordinary! It's perfect workshop material and a great combination of focused information, inspiring messages, and practical material."
~ **Shama Viola**, Ambassador and Teacher, Damanhuir Community, Italy

TESTIMONIALS

"Wow, what a wonderful read! A compelling argument and, perhaps more importantly, framework for a purpose-driven future for individuals, communities, and companies alike. The New Story totally resonated. I particularly appreciated the discussions of the roles. After years of exploration and trying things on instinct, it is so nice to see recognition and definition of my type of role - "Creative catalyst" is exactly what I am!"
~ **BeiBei Song**, Chief Creative Officer, Essinova, and Executive Coach, Stanford Graduate School of Business

"A brilliant read for finding our work passion in changing times. So many ask, what is the work of transformation and how do I navigate it? Although we feel the transformation the full meaning alludes us. Whitney and Charlie do a great job of describing what's happening. Importantly, how our worldview and beliefs are slowly transitioning from industrialization to promoting community and a sustainable way of life for all." ~
~ **Jayne Heggen**, Founder of Heggen Group LLC

"Work The Future! Today redefines how we commit to the greater good through our work now. It provides an embraceable framework for businesses to move from an egocentric, short sighted profit model to a shared purpose, sustainable model for true long-term benefit. A core culture of benefit that will create multiple profit centers. Early adopters will have a unique advantage in the marketplace."
~ **Leili McKinley**, Founder, Identitype Group, and Guest Lecturer at Tufts University

"The future is far too important to wait until tomorrow."

TABLE OF CONTENTS

WorkTheFuture Today

INTRODUCTION

The Future (of Work) Isn't Working

We live in an increasingly purposeless world filled with purposeless work—but there's always hope and help if you know where to find it. That's why we wrote this book: To give you hope and show you that help is at hand.

The Old Story of Profit First and its attendant social institutions were designed to promote continuous growth at any cost; first through extraction of non-renewable resources, later by industrial efficiency, now through manipulation of financial systems—and always through corruption and cronyism.

Old Story institutions are no longer supportive of personal well-being, the integration of body, mind, and spirit, let alone human wholeness, the integration of individuals into a greater community. Work is a central human activity that can provide sustenance, identity, and community, as well as a sense of purpose.

The New Story of Purpose First is about life affirmation and planetary sustainability. The New Story is emerging. But right now we are feeling the pangs of birth; the struggle to leave the womb and breathe on it's own. You can be part of that New

Story. But first, you have to throw off the Old Story thinking; let go of limiting attitudes so you can embrace a new sense of shared purpose and possibility. We have some ideas and thoughts about how to do all that. We invite you to be part of the New Story of Purpose First.

Purpose: Finding Your **Why?** Your Guiding North Star.

Shared purpose is the social-psychological glue that binds humans together. It includes a commonly held belief system, which informs our attitudes and ultimately our behavior. Why is purpose important now? Purpose is important because humankind has reached a point in its evolution where it can consciously choose its guiding principle: creation or destruction.

Why Purpose?

Purpose is the Why of our Whys. All humans are in and on a purpose quest, whether they know it or not. The sole purpose of human existence is ultimately our soul purpose, which raises the questions:

- **Why are we here?**
- **What are we to do?**

We are here to find our purpose and the corresponding path to its fulfillment so that we may become better together. Life is about what we are becoming. It is about turning this into that, and what matters most is not the this or the that, but:

- the into, the transition, because shift happens constantly,
- the emotional experience of transformation through creation, recreation, and conflict co-resolution, and
- the movement from fear to love, from me to we, and from anger and angst to amity and abundance.

Why Now?

The New Story of Purpose First needs to be started to take the place of the Old Story, and shared for the salvation of our souls, livelihoods, and planet. The Old Story of Why are we here? (endless expansion) and What are we to do? (exploit the planet and each other) is a huge dying liability, and has no replacement. We are in dire need of the New Story of how to get out of this big fat mess we are mired in, and to start on the path to transformation so we may become better together through individual and shared positive purpose, and an awakening to our shared wholeness and inescapable mutuality.

The power of the old myths—sold to the masses and perpetuated by America's rich powerful elite (the one percent) for generations—is dying.

21

The Old Story was built on top of a number of other myths such as Manifest Destiny, Westward Ho!, the Rugged Frontiersman, the Lone Cowboy, the Self-Made Man, and the American Dream. From 1950 to 1975 this dream became a reality for more than not as the postwar boom, based on American global supremacy, provided a rising tide that lifted many boats.

By 1980, the 1950s myths of Infinite Growth, Everybody Can Become Middle Class, and The Business of America is Business, collectively known as the American Dream, turned into the American Nightmare on Main Street. These myths have not been replaced, so we are operating in a vacuum without a compass.

We need to give birth to a new philosophy constructed upon shared positive purpose, values, and value; rethinking Profit, People, Planet; and creating a new pathway to creating a new socially forward story—Planet, People, Profit.

Why Work? And What's the Purpose of Work?

Some have asked us Why focus on work? Because the very nature of work as we have known it for several hundred years is changing, and that is driving other profound changes in the rest of our lives.

What do we hope to accomplish with our perspective on the New Story of Purpose First? Bottom line, we seek to:

- Awaken concerned people to their need to re/discover their Purpose, Place, and Practice for sharing that purpose.
- Provide them with a pathway for discovering their purpose, particularly in the workplace.
- Address how civic leaders can create community purpose.

The workplace is where so many people spend so much time doing things they really don't like and don't want to. They often don't understand the purpose–the why–of what they're asked, directed, and forced into doing. They work hard and achieve little, or hardly work.

Stories: **Telling and Selling**

Stories and narratives are important because they are the basis of your culture and brand. We tell our stories not as an end in itself, but as an attempt to liberate ourselves from them, to evolve and grow well beyond them.

We tell our stories to:

- transform ourselves;
- to learn about our past and share our experiences to transcend them;
- to use our stories to make a positive difference in our world;
- to broaden our point-of-view to see beyond our daily routines;

- to act beyond a story that might have incapacitated us;
- and to live out more of our spiritual and earthly potential.

As the Old Story of Profit First is coming to an end, and we need a New Story of Purpose First to take us across the chasm of change so we can become better together and nurture all life on our small planet through shared stories and the power they have to transform people.

WTF! What's The Transformation? What needs to happen?
The Old Story was about Profit First, of endless exploitation and expansion, and is coming to an end. Our world has lost its way and has no core purpose, along with our misleaders and misleading institutions. Our worldview and beliefs were built upon massive industrialization and commercialization that is unsustainable, and does not promote a sense of community and a sustainable way of life for all. Many people are in denial that the crumbling of our society has begun. But you don't have to look much further than the news media to find stark evidence of this happening.

The New York Times recently reported:

"Suicide in the United States has surged to the highest levels in nearly 30 years, a federal data analysis has found, with increases in every age group except older adults. The rise was particularly steep for women. It was also substantial among middle-aged Americans, sending a signal of deep anguish from a group whose suicide rates had been stable or falling since the 1950s."

WTF! What's The Future? What just happened?

Guess what? Shift happens. And in case you didn't notice… it just happened again… on a y-u-g-e scale. Irreversibly so. Change is often highly unpredictable but it can and does happen. All the time. The old ways of being and doing. Over. So what are you going to do about securing your future, today? What's the future of your Business? Stakeholders? Community? Local government? They're all highly vulnerable. We're here to Work The Future! Today with you to help you and your stakeholders move away from the old and toward the new world of *both opportunity and uncertainty*.

**"TOMORROW is far too important
to be left to the FUTURE–
we've got to SEIZE THE DAY."**

25

"The future depends on what you do today."

OWNER'S MANUAL

Work The Future! Today
Finding your path to purpose, passion and profit

Three steps to *unleashing* your potential.
By Whitney Vosburgh + Charlie Grantham

WORK THE FUTURE! TODAY INTRODUCES
THE ART OF THE POSSIBLE, PRACTICED WELL IN ADVANCE.

It was thoughts like this that led us to write this book together throughout 2016. Since the stories we tell ourselves and each other frame the worlds we believe in and live in, and the Old Story of Profit First is coming to an end, we need a New Story of Purpose First to take us across the chasm of change, chaos, and complexity to a brand new, culture-built, forward-facing world—where we can nurture all life on our small planet through shared transformative emotional exchanges and experiences.

So what's your story for 2018 and beyond?

27

A Manifesto for the 21st Century: There are three parts to our book "Work The Future! Today: Finding the path to purpose, passion and profit".

Part 1: Purpose We look at the Old Story of Profit First, which has given us a direction that isn't working, and the New Story of Purpose First, which is still being born.
Part 2: Place We describe how crossing the chasm between old and new is going to require people to get clear on personal purpose, and we link that to the purposes of their workplace and larger social community.
Part 3: Practice We offer direction for how you begin to live this New Story, the practice for making this happen.

This book is a pathway, with signposts toward the New Story via Purpose, Place, and Practice.

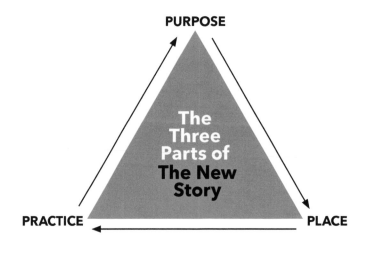

PURPOSE

The
Three
Parts of
**The New
Story**

PRACTICE

PLACE

The New Story of Purpose First must replace the Old Story of Profit First.
We need a new illuminating North Star to guide our journey towards well-being.
We must give birth to a new philosophy constructed upon shared positive purpose
and value, and that means rethinking Profit, People, Planet, and creating a new
pathway to building a new thriving story and reality—Planet, People, Profit.

Why is this transition through positive and powerful transformation important now?
Because humankind has reached a point in its evolution where it can consciously choose
between creation and destruction. Our goal is to participate in the birth of the New Story.
If you knew what tomorrow would look like, what would you be doing today? The
future is far too important to wait until tomorrow—we must work the future, today.

Innovation vs. Transformation? All Part of a Spectrum
Acting as a trusted advisor to our clients, we provide a pathway of best practices
tailored to meet people and organizations where they can make best uses of what

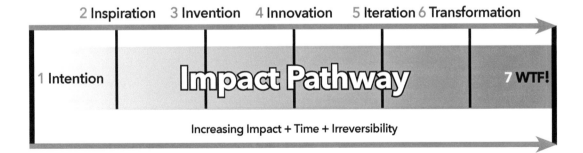

we offer. Overall, there is a foundation to our offering that over time increases our impact and eventually the change we help create becomes irreversible.

The steps of our Impact Pathway that we follow, in order, are:

1. **Define intention**
2. **Create inspiration**
3. **Catalyze invention**
4. **Apply innovation**
5. **Improve through iteration**
6. **Perform transformation**
7. **Realize Work The Future!**

What's Your Moon Shot? Looked at another way, our seven-step pathway starts with purpose, moves onto branding through culture re/creation to brand re/creation so that you can follow your illuminating and guiding North Star's trajectory all along your pathway to your defining Moon Shot. We'd love to work with you to find your trajectory.

There is no today, the here and now, without yesterday and tomorrow. There is no now, without before and later. They're all relative to one another and we're all similarly related… in relationship to one another and the planet we share—our only planet—of which we are an inseparable part. So, here's how we work the future today to build a better future together.

Know Now, or Now How

To enjoy a better future together, we must start working together, today, to co-create a better future together. As the future is a series of todays, of new nows, we must co-create that new, better now by asking How can we start, now? And since we share an inescapable web of mutuality, we need to work together to create a better future together.

Innovate Today, Transform Tomorrow

Innovation is about a better today, whereas transformation is about a better tomorrow, so we must innovate but we must, more importantly, transform the past, today, and tomorrow into a better future for all of us by collaborating and co-creating shared and aligned purpose and value to create a future that we will value today, tomorrow, and long into the future.

The Heart of the Matter

So, we must always ask ourselves: What are we right now? What is it that we wish to become next, soon, later, much later, and long into the future? It is this transitional state that is the heart of the matter. As we all know, the future matters because if we don't act intentionally then the future will happen but probably not in the way we want it to.

Embrace Y/our Future!

We have the power to shape the future while dancing with uncertainty, ambiguity, and constant change, along with embracing the chaos, confusion, and complexity that come with it. We need to know what our being is based on—which purpose and values—and then, having a clear idea of what our gift to the world is, share it and enjoy a sense of direction and purpose, a North Star to point the way.

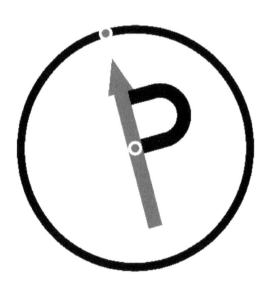

WTF! **Manifesto:** To awaken concerned people to the importance of reaping

the rewards of re/discovering their Purpose (the why of their lives and the gift/s

they have to offer themselves and others), their Place (with whom and where

to best share it), and their Practice (how and when to best share it).

33

"Control your own destiny or someone else will."

PART I – PURPOSE

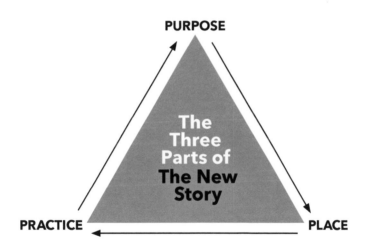

PART I – PURPOSE

Chapter 1: **This Into That**

Different stages of life need different stories. We have *never* seen anything like the world we're moving towards today.

Today we live in a purposeless world. Some of us often feel like the Dark Side is in control, even if we can't always define just want we mean by the dark side. At work,

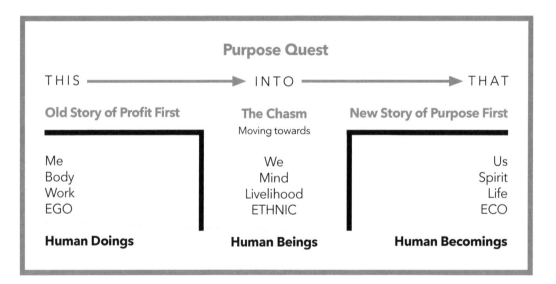

we are under-led and over-managed. In the home, consumerism reigns supreme and our communities are governed by near feudal politics. And yet, we hope for better things to come. We have written this book as a first step towards people enjoying a common shared purpose—and realizing their truest selves as a result.

"We are caught in an inescapable network of mutuality, tied in a single garment of destiny. Whatever affects one directly, affects all indirectly."
~ Martin Luther King, Jr.

As it has so often, humanity is breaking away from the past—and pulling the future towards us. We are in a chasm between the this and the that. We call this the process of moving from the Old Story of Profit First into the New Story of Purpose First.

This book began as a series of blogs focused on bringing shared purpose to work. That series was embedded in a far larger idea of which work is only a part—although a major part—of our lives. The pathway, on which we are inviting you to join us, is about evolving into a global society whose goal is becoming better together. Our shared purpose on that path is to harmoniously promote the well-being of everyone and the life systems we all benefit from—and of which we are an inseparable part.

For Whitney, the journey to this book started with the need to revisit his purpose periodically and reinvent himself accordingly. His children moved out and his curiosity

SIDEBAR

Old Story ⟶	New Story
Fear	Love
Anger	Acceptance
Space	Place
House	Home
Greed	Generosity
Scarcity	Abundance
Confusion	Clarity
Denial of Death	Embrace of Life
EGO	LET GO

Shift Happens: New Symbols of Meaning

This is deeper than a mere shift in economic systems, or political philosophies. It is deeply symbolic, which gets expressed in our stories. We will spare you the deep psychoanalysis, but suffice to say that in Jungian archetypal terms, we are in the midst of moving from a dominant 'male' image of stern father control to one more 'female,' which emphasizes nurturance. In our contemporary American culture, we see it as a symbolic change from John Wayne to Ophrah Winfrey. Ultimately, we see shifting from a focus on "he" to "she" to "we".

moved back in, and he found himself asking: Who am I, now? Out of this came re-search for a book titled *Second Act: Creating a meaningful middle age and beyond*, Whitney's transition to divinity school where he studied community-building, and starting Brand New Purpose, a brand transformation consultancy that creates pur-pose-built, values-driven strategies and solutions.

Charlie found himself actually walking the pathway and making the transition from the Old Story to the New Story before he was aware that's what he was doing. The experience led him to start a practice, *Awakening to Wholeness*, aimed at helping people and communities make the same transition. We hope to share with you what we have learned on our separate and now shared journeys. *Thank you for joining us.*

Well-Being

Well-being or wellness is a general term for the condition of an individual or group, pertaining to their social, economic, psychological, spiritual or medical state. A high level of well-being means in some sense the individual or group's condition is posi-tive, while low well-being is a negative condition.

We use well-being and wellness interchangeably to refer to a spiritual as much as a physical state. Well-being cannot exist just in your head. It combines feeling good with actually having meaning, nurturing relationships, and feeling a sense of accomplishment:

"Wellness is not a medical fix but a way of living—a lifestyle sensitive and responsive to all the dimensions of body, mind, and spirit, an approach to life we each design to achieve our highest potential for well-being now and forever." ~ Greg Anderson

Wellness and Work

Old Story institutions are no longer life-affirming, supportive of personal well-being (integration of body, mind, and spirit), nor conducive to the integration of individuals into a greater whole, as we are all one.

Work is a central human activity, which provides livelihood, community, identity, and we now realize, well-being and wholeness. We first focused on work because it is universal—irrespective of political affiliation, religion or culture. We spend more time working than anything else, except perhaps sleeping. It is what demands our immediate attention. In Western society, we often base our personal identities on our work. And to most people who are not fully aware of what well-being and wholeness mean, work remains their only purpose. Like so many other outmoded social institutions and norms, work for many has become dysfunctional and pulled our humanity into a dark pit of hopelessness.

Why is purpose important now? Humankind has reached a point in its evolution where it can consciously choose between creation or destruction. We have a choice: Is it going to be global warming, warning, or warring? Or, love, peace, and prosperity for all?

Why Purpose?

For most of us, our purpose comes from work. But purpose is larger than that. Purpose is the Why of our Whys. And quest comes before questions. All humans are in and on a purpose quest, whether they know it or not. Our sole purpose, human existence, is ultimately our soul purpose, which answers these questions:

• Why are we here?
• What are we here to do?

Why Now?

The New Story of Purpose needs to be started to take the place of the Old Story of Profit. It needs to be shared for the salvation of our souls, livelihoods, and planet. The Old Story of Profit First—of endless exploitation and expansion—is a huge, dying liability. We are in dire need of The New Story of Purpose First, of meaningfulness for people, and prosperity for all. We need to start on the path to positive transformation:

• So we may become better together through positive individual and shared purpose,
• So we may share our values and unique gifts with one another,
• So we may awaken to our shared wholeness and inescapable mutuality, as we're all in it together.

The potency of the old myth—sold to the masses and perpetuated for generations by America's rich, powerful elite, and their minions—is dying.

The myth was built on top of a number of other myths such as Manifest Destiny, Westward Ho!, the Rugged Frontiersman, the Lone Cowboy, the Self-Made Man, and the American Dream. This dream became a reality for more than not from 1950 to 1975 as the postwar boom, based on American global supremacy, provided a rising tide that lifted many boats.

However, the unlimited growth was an exception to the arc of history and came to a crashing halt. By 1980, the intertwined myths of Infinite Growth, of Everybody Can Become Middle Class, and of The Business of America is Business, collectively known as the American Dream of Wall Street, turned into the American Nightmare on Main Street. These myths have not been replaced, so we are operating in a vacuum without a compass and, at best, going nowhere. At worst, we are going somewhere we don't want to go and from which there is no return. It's like flying blind with no compass, gas gauge or altimeter against strong headwinds in a pea soup fog.

In sum, because the world has lost its way and has no core purpose, along with its misleaders and misleading institutions, we need a new illuminating North Star to guide our journey—The New Story of Purpose of being better together. Our world view and beliefs were built upon massive industrialization and commercialization that are no longer able to promote a life-affirming sense of community and co-existence, and are unsustainable.

We need to give birth to a new philosophy constructed upon shared positive purpose and value, which means rethinking profit–people–planet, and creating a new pathway to building a new socially forward story and reality, such as planet–people–profit. Without a healthy planet, there would be no healthy people and no healthy profits, for sure, which is why we put planet ahead of people.

As all humans seek meaning, we are all mapmakers and in pursuit of the pathway to purpose. We say pathway–the way of the path–because a path emerges from use over time. A path is useful from the start, whereas a road may or may not be. A path is found and co-determined by its users from inception, whereas a road is designed and pre-determined by its builders–and then it might be used or not.

The old story was about roads to nowhere. The new one will be about pathways to possibility, plenty, and purpose.

What we hope to accomplish with this book:

• To awaken concerned people to the importance of reaping the rewards of re/discovering their Purpose (the why of their lives—the gift they have to offer themselves and others), their Place (with whom and where to best share it), and their Practice (how to best share it).

• Provide them with a pathway to accomplish that in life, in the workplace, and in their communities.

The Pathway of This Book

This diagram shows a purposeful pathway for you to use as you read through our book. Come back to it often to see where you have been, where you are, and where we will lead you to next.

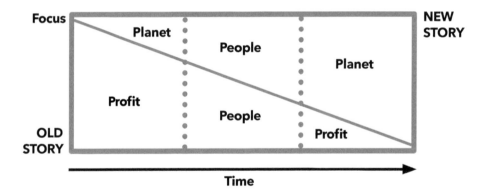

Finally, the world is experiencing a mega-shift, a move from profit as a prime motivator to active concern for the well-being of the entire planet and all of us sharing that purpose.

"Can't solve problems with the thinking that created them."

PART I – PURPOSE

Chapter 2: **What's Your Why? And Why Is That?**

Backstory

Let's dig in. As our chapter title says, there are two major things to talk about now: What's your why? And Why is that? Think about it like a Zen koan, which is a philosophical riddle. The questions don't have any quick right or wrong answers. They stop the linear thinking process of the Old Story, and offer you the chance to slow down and absorb the whole idea of Why?

We took this question of "What's your why?" to a group of friends and acquaintances early on. Two things came out of that research that we felt deserved some in-depth discussion. First, we wanted to explore why answering the Why question is so hard for some. Second, we wanted to clarify an apparent mismatch between personal purpose in our life, and purpose in our livelihood. After our report from the field, we offer up our ideas on answers to those two questions.

Our Survey: Reach Out and Touch Someone

When we started this journey down the pathway to purpose, we held many assumptions. Being thoughtful, studious types, we thought we had the whole purpose thing figured out. Well, not so much. Realizing it was time for a reality check, we reached out to a short list of our friends, acquaintances, and people we thought shared our interest in finding purpose in life. Boy, were we surprised at what we found.

People answered questions designed to test our own ideas and thoughts. What we present here is a summary of the responses we received. There was much confirmation for our assumptions, but some new insights as well. We used this knowledge to improve, structure, and guide our work.

What is Purpose?

In short, purpose is the answer to the question "What's the why of your life?" People see purpose as the general orienting idea of their lives—their guiding North Star. While people have different ways to express it, generally they define purpose as being in this world. It's authentic. It's about intention. The best quote of those we received:

"Purpose is the reason for being—a calling. It's the embodiment of one's voice in service of the whole."

Recognizing that this is still a very high level concept, we sought to understand what purpose isn't.

What is Purpose Not?

Succinctly, our colleagues told us that anything associated with doing, particularly if motivated by a desire or need for compensation and acknowledgment, is not purpose. Task-oriented, reactive behavior often doesn't take us in the direction of embodying our voice in the service of the whole. The reigning symbol of purpose-lessness is Dilbert—Charlie should know, as he actually worked with the original Dilbert in real life when he and Scott Adams shared an employer.

People saw work almost as an antithesis of purpose; a world of tag lines, vague mission statements, traditional corporate-controlled lives—not purpose-driven engagement that truly brought them meaning. We were aware that our sample meant we inevitably missed people for whom work is deeply fulfilling. Still, our findings were instructive. As one respondent put it:

Non-purpose is characterized by "self-absorption, thoughtlessness, and materialism."

Why Now?

Eighty percent of the people we surveyed found purpose to be important to them. And when asked "Why now?" they suspected it had something to do with maturity—it was not necessarily age-related. Some had found an interest in purpose because of a life-changing event, others through a slowly evolving need to be anchored in something greater than themselves. As one of them said:

"Without Purpose, there is emptiness. There would be little value to life; no direction, no markers of success, and no accountability."

One respondent put it even more succinctly, saying:

"Purpose is what being alive is all about."

Purpose of Life

We also explored the metaphysical: "What is the purpose of life?" Participants told us it means to maximize well-being for self and, more importantly, for others—to find true meaning. A small portion, about 10%, sees purpose as fulfilling the biological imperative to continue the species and thrive. And there was one courageous individual who took the words right out of our mouths, observing that the purpose of life is:

"To help the evolution of consciousness."

What's Your Purpose?

What about you? People turned out to be quite thoughtful here. Maybe the process of looking inward produced insights participants hadn't known they had. One respondent said her purpose was to:

"Bring spirit to ground, love, and learning."

One surprise was discovering that people were conscious of not engaging with others who didn't have a purpose, or a shared purpose. For everyone, purpose came through as some variant on simply "Being in this world." We'd call it being present. And in support of our suspicion that in today's world there is a major disconnect between individual (life) and livelihood (work) purpose, we got:

"My purpose is to help people who have lost theirs—particularly in their place of work."

Purpose + Place
One of our key constructs is that purpose needs a space to be acted out. We believe that people act out purpose and experience purpose as they interact with the world around them, and in them. Think of space as a physical location; whereas place is the physical plus your social identity. It might help to think of space as like a house and place as like a home.

Some of our participants did think of spaces in their communities, which could be made into places. Commonly they offered church and communal common areas as spaces to live out purpose by transforming them from spaces to places. They saw these transformed spaces as somewhere to connect their life to a larger social group. In so doing, they transformed the space to a place, and were able to experience purpose through it.

What Would You Do to Make a Space a Place?

When we asked this question, the answer we got most often was people would make a space into a place by doing something to consciously engage in community interaction—collaboration based on shared purpose and values. This collaboration is not something that just happens on its own. It takes intentional action by more than one person. It's not surprising that this fits with the research on social change: We know that it takes a small group; say ten, to begin to effect social change. As Peter Block, a community guru, wrote:

"The small group is the unit of transformation." and

"Bring people together in conversation to imagine and create possibilities."

What Do You Do to Live Out Your Purpose?

The responses to this question were so rich we turned them into a word cloud.

How Do You Spend Your Time?

We asked a subset of our respondents how they invested their time. Did they spend it doing things, experiencing emotions (being), or in service of something greater

than themselves? They told us (multiple responses were allowed, so the numbers don't add up to 100%):

- 57% doing things
- 37% emotions and/or being
- 34% in service

Clearly, we have a long way to go to get behaviors to match intention, given the high value people say they put on being and being in service. People spend much more time just doing. We are not human doings; we are human beings in the process of becoming.

What Gets in the Way?

What gets in the way of people achieving their desire for being? We were amazed that only one-third of people answered this question. This deserves more research. Here are the top answers. People say these things get in the way of them achieving their desire for being: ego, everyday distractions, fear, self-doubt, working for money.

Planet–People–Profit?

Another of our key assumptions is that we are witnessing a significant shift away from the Old Story, where human life was dominated by a drive toward profit, to one that is driven toward nurturing one another and being stewards of our planet. Our respondents confirmed this. When asked what was most important to them, they responded:

- 52% people
- 36% planet
- 8% profit
- 4% "huh?"

We'll further explore the process of this shift later. Now we have all this valuable data and a framework to express our ideas. Why should it matter to you?

"The future ain't what it used to be." We used to plan for it. Now, we're overwhelmed by it. Thinking about "So what?" forces us to consider what the right plan could be. Time to change. But plan around what? What should be our focus? Plan for what?

People and organizations need to have a purpose to make sense of their existence and give it meaning—an operating system, so to speak, as well as a guiding North Star.

We need to go from a mean focus on profit to meaning, and from gloom about how we can live a life of purpose to bloom. It's time for Purpose with a capital "P"—and for a way to put it to work to create a better, more meaningful future by starting today. To predict the future with purpose is to invent the future today. We call it working the future, today.

Why is the Why So Hard?

One of the great pieces of feedback we got in our Purpose Quest/ionnaire was that thinking about, let alone practicing, purpose was very difficult for many people. We wondered why. Here's what we think.

54

Thinking about, discovering, and working on Purpose requires us to do some things we normally don't engage with. First, there is intention. That means really paying attention to the present moment.

For some, that's a loaded word. What do you intend to do tomorrow? What are you intending to do right now? That's hard. Our minds wander; we get overwhelmed with all kinds of things like noise, visuals, smells, memories, and other kinds of distractions. Intention means consciously directing your energy—physical, emotional and intellectual—towards a specific goal or action. Think of it as focused awareness. Focus on a target. Focus on Purpose to discover your why, the why of your existence, your life.

How many people spend a measurable amount of time doing that? This is the first problem with working on Purpose: You need to be intent to do it.

Only one-third of our questionnaire respondents could articulate what got in their way of being purposeful. We suspect lack of intention, of focus, is a big barrier.

The second major reason why Purpose is so hard is psychological. Humans love illusions, distractions, and delays. They keep us from having to deal with our emotions, to admit our existence is full of painful experiences.

When you begin to explicitly deal with your Purpose, painful feelings may confront you. What most of us do is sidestep those emotions, pretending they don't exist and locking them up in a little corner of our minds with the thought: "Oh, it's okay, I'll get to it later."

That defense mechanism is called spiritual bypass. It happens when we get into spiritual distractions as a way of not dealing with unpleasantries. One of Charlie's mentors has a not-so-polite way of referring to those engaged in spiritual bypass: bliss parrots. These are people who attend weekend retreats or seminars and come back "enlightened," spewing forth all kinds of love and light messages that they are simply regurgitating without understanding them.

You've seen them. You run into them at social events and they just won't stop talking about Rama Lama Ding Dong and his/her seven principles of true divineness. Bliss parrots. Another example of folks who are engaged in spiritual bypass is friends who find out that you are walking the pathway of awakening and want you to tell them three quick ways to achieve wholeness. When you start to seriously engage in conversations with them about Purpose, you usually get three responses in this order:

1. I'm going to have to work on this?
2. I'm scared!
3. My ego doesn't like this.

Now, most of this will be covered up with all kinds of magical thinking, rationalizations, and excuses. But, right there, you have found a lightweight. You have run right smack into their barriers to finding their Purpose.

Don't be a bliss parrot or a lightweight. Focus your awareness, wrap yourself around it, and get on with it. After all, we have only fear to fear.

The Gap Between You and Your Work

The other thing that jumped out at us from our Purpose Quest was an absence of people talking about how their work—their livelihood, in Buddhist thought—helped them live out their individual purpose. We expected that, but here was evidence that this is a fact of modern life. We were gratified to be able to share with our colleagues the explosion of work on purpose, generally and in the workplace, in the past few years.

So, if we are talking about Shared Purpose becoming the New Story, it's important that folks aren't seeing that in their work lives. Why is this? Because the very nature of work as we have known it for several hundred years is changing—and that is driving other profound changes in the rest of our lives.

When personal purpose and organizational purpose are not aligned and supportive of one another, doubt, despair, and dysfunction begin to set in. And that is exactly where many people are today.

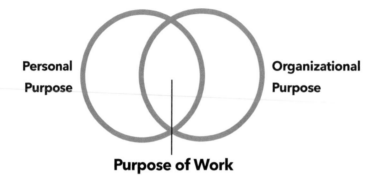

Personal Purpose

Organizational Purpose

Purpose of Work

If you agree with our contention that we are shifting from a world of profit to a world of planet and people, it may be that this Purpose Gap is a leading indicator of things to come. Let's look at why this gap could explain some of the madness and mayhem that seems to have overtaken the planet.

Purpose, Attitudes, and Behavior Explained

When a person's purpose and their work don't align, there's a conflict. The conflict creates FUD (Fear, Uncertainty, and Doubt). Struggling with this inner conflict eats up mental and emotional energy. People often try to resolve this conflict by focusing on their power, their status, or their income.

Different reactions emerge depending on whether people see the disconnect between purpose and work as their fault or the fault of others. For example, if you think your purpose is right and noble, but your workplace is not, you might feel aggression toward your workplace. If you believe you are at fault, you might begin engaging in self-destructive behaviors.

Neither is a positive outcome. In each case, you are turned off. You must move out of the disconnect to resolve the conflict. Next time you see a report of violence in the workplace, take a deeper look at what was going on.

Let's take a simple example. Let's say:

• A person's purpose is helping those in need: the poor and the planet.
• An employer's purpose is to generate profit without regard to environmental impact.

A person's purpose and that of their employer are at odds. The person doesn't feel he/she has the power to create alignment. This results in rebelliousness. Look for a trip down the hall to the traditional "dehumanizing resources department."

This disconnect is what we think operates in most of today's workplaces. Where we are today is not good for people, or, for that matter, for the companies making a profit from people's labor.

Wrapping It Up

We started out by looking at "What's your why?" and "Why is that?" We shared a summary of the highlights from our research that asked these questions of engaged people. What we found that the why of life is about the experience of being present in this world, not just doing something.

Finding a place to work on purpose and live it out seemed to be a difficult concept for our participants. We didn't think that would be the case but there it is. So, we are going to devote considerable effort to explaining that later in this book.

People also told us that they were mystified about what got in their way to being more purposeful. We get in our own way. We found that people spend almost twice as much time doing things as they do putting energy into being, including sharing their gifts with others.

We talked about creating a world that is rapidly shifting to a planet/people focus. Next, we spent some time looking at the psychology of the mismatch of people's personal purpose (being) and their work (doing). We hope the patterns we've uncovered have helped you make sense of much of current day bizarreness.

Next, we stay with the me theme to look at "So, what's your story?" You've got your purpose down. You've got a plan to live it out. You can get around what's in your way. Now what? What authentic role do you play on this world's stage? What's your personal, heartfelt script?

The most important thing is to know that most of us are living in both the Old Story and the New Story simultaneously. Every one of us has a unique path and combinations of the old and new within. What truly counts is what happens in and to us when we are in between stories. If you are reading this book, that's likely exactly where you are. You're experiencing the transition between the two where the alchemical gold of who you truly are and what gift you bring to life is found… questions, not answers… searching, not certainty.

'Tis the quest. As soon as we reach our destination, it is time to reach out to our next. Take a deep breath and turn the page.

"The eyes of the future are looking back at us and praying."

PART I – PURPOSE

Chapter 3: **So, What's Your Story?**

The brand new purpose of Purpose is to turn me into we and then we into us. Me is singular. We is plural. Us is inclusively plural, as in the USA: the United States of All.

Your core purpose and values are the heart and lungs of what makes you unique. They bring your essence to life. The next question to address once you've identified your core purpose and values is: What is my purpose-built, values-driven story? Later, we ask: What shall I do about and with my story?

What you value is what is more important to you than anything else. It is typically what you focus on. First comes your Why? As in: Why am I on this planet? That's your purpose. Then comes: What qualities illuminate and guide the expression of my purpose? Those are your core values that lie at the heart of your story along with your purpose. Core values can also be called your passion. Values are emotional. Purpose is more rational. To put it another way, purpose is of the head and passion is of the heart. And as the head turns, the body follows, which is why purpose leads values.

Got your purpose figured out? Okay, so what's your story? What's your thirty-second elevator pitch? What's your five-minute cocktail conversation? That's what this chapter is about—connecting your story with your community of stakeholders, the people who value you, at the right place and time—telling your story so you can be sharing your unique value, your gift with the world.

Below are our thoughts on how this shift from profit to people to planet impacts your story. Then you have your purpose and your story, and can discover the right role for yourself in the world.

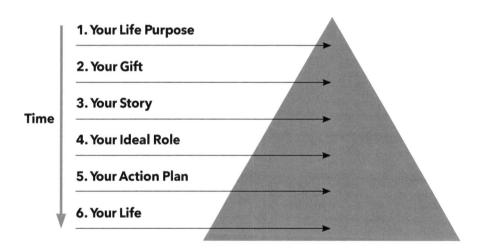

Six Steps to a Purposeful Life

Your brand is the living, breathing emotional relationship you have with yourself and with others. It is important to realize that your brand is what others perceive it to be. You can tell and live out your story. But, do others experience it that way? Do they believe it is your authentic essence? If not, you are telling your story, but you might not be selling it through your deeds—walking your talk.

Given that, What is your brand, and how does your story reflect it? Your brand story is that short, to-the-point narrative that tells the world what your purpose is, what your values are, and what is the unique value, your gift, you intend to share with others—the we and ultimately the us.

We live in a world where everything is interrelated and forever changing. We are in transition. So, when you tell your story, you should think about the answers to these questions: What is your Old Story? And your New Story? How are you transitioning from one to the other? Where are you in the chasm between the two stories? How do you know when you've arrived on the other side?

What Values Do You Stand For?
Most people have a set of core values. What are your core values based on your purpose? What are you focused on? How do these values come to life? What impact do your values have?

As our world shifts from a core value of profit to a core value of caring for the planet and its people, several trends have merged. About a decade ago, people started talking about a "triple bottom line" for business: Profit–People–Planet. But notice that it is business jargon, and profit, of course, comes first. We don't think that we have the best grammar and vocabulary to talk about this subtle shift, yet. But we need new people-friendly lingo for sure. Bear with us and let's look at what your core values are. What's your personal triple bottom line?

The triple bottom line measures not only financial performance (profit); but incorporates reliable measures of environmental impact (planet) and community impact (people). It brings together what traditionally was called economic and community development and sustainability. Where do you fit in these three aspects of value?

Our point is that for long-term sustainability in a social system, you need to consider three major factors: people, planet, and profit. Each of them is necessary, but on their own none of them is sufficient for balance. We are also offering the assertion that in the past (the Old Story) profit was overwhelmingly the primary goal and that now we are seeing a shift toward planet. If we put this into a visual image, it looks like three overlapping areas of concern. When people and profit intersect, you get equitable results; profit and planet overlaps are viable; people and planet gives you bearable results. However, you only obtain sustainability when all three are equally balanced.

Shared Purpose + Sustainability

Investment in the environment includes the community where things are made, but also those places in the earth that provide our resources.

Investment in social capital refers to the exchange of value within the social network where we live, work, and play. More broadly, social capital is the value of social relationships and networks—who you know who knows others—that can be used to create win-win relationships, situations, and experiences that act as a social glue to help people become and stay better together. Social capital is a tangible asset you have control over. Is social capital part of your story? We will return to this idea in chapters 8, 9, and 10 when we talk about the "Us."

We must get beyond an accounting discussion to make the transition from the Old Story to the New Story. B Corps, which are for-profit companies certified to meet rigorous standards of social and environmental performance, accountability, and transparency, are increasingly popular precisely because they represent an accounting system that includes social capital.

Personal Triple Bottom Line

Here's a look at a possible personal triple bottom line:

The What	Standard for Comparison	Description
Planet	Environmental Impacts	Currently measures the lessening of "bad" impacts such as reducing carbon footprint, recycling, etc. Moving towards future-focused preservation and recycling, reuse, and re-purposing of resources.
People	Social Capital	Measures people's increasing capability (what you can do today) and capacity (your potential to do even more tomorrow, with the proper guidance and support) to share their purpose and gifts with the larger "us." Includes quality of life and things like "Gross Happiness Index," which is an alternative to GDP.
Profit	Standard Financials	Commonly seen as "compensation" in monetary terms. In the New Story, extended to the larger and overall community, including measures of common wealth.

> The emergence of the triple bottom line in business is a sign that the one-dimensional Old Story of Profit First is being replaced by a new multi-dimensional value system that focuses on and measures what all people value—as they do in Sweden—not just a controlling minority.

This idea of the triple bottom line is gathering steam. Businesses that are annually certified as "B Corp" have their performances tracked using their triple bottom line, and "Benefit Companies" have their missions to benefit stakeholders beyond shareholders clearly written into their incorporation papers.

Milton Friedman's economic theory of the supremacy of monetary profit, the myth that Wall Street used in the last century to justify the perpetuation of the Old Story, is slowly dying.

Sounds good? So how do you focus on the new triple bottom line? First, you need a totally open and publicly available bookkeeping system so everyone in the community knows what is happening. And yes, that includes salaries, benefits, and total compensation. As each person is unique, each market is different, so there is a social contract negotiation process about the value of participants' commonly held shared values. What is the value of the social glue that binds people together?

We need a new system to track who is contributing what, and what we collectively get in return. More creative people living the New Story are looking at things like increases in quality of life and social support in addition to more traditional measures (cash, volunteer time, commitment to service) for all they impact.

All the World's a Stage—What Is Your Calling in Life?

The first part of your story is your purpose. The middle part to your story is about the values you hold sacred and how you know when you are living those out. The last part is about how that all comes into being: How your purpose and story are perceived, what people see you doing in the act of sharing, and what you are sharing.

We value things that come in threes. We talk about the body, mind, and spirit. These are the three legs of the stool of the roles we act out in everyday life. These are not rigid roles. They're more like an invitation to participate in an improvisation within a given context.

We like the idea of improvisational acting. Part of practicing your role may lie in learning how to be improvisational. Ever been part of a role-play guided by an experienced facilitator? They're a great learning experience.

Back to specific role-playing in the world of the New Story. The three-legged stool of body, mind, and spirit has a strong parallel in the work world from which we are emerging. In the language of the Old Story, at work we call people executives, man-agers, and the catch-all category we call creative catalysts. We suggest some subtle changes in the language that describes social roles.

The Old Story celebrated the strong father-knows-best image. Leaders were pro-jecting this image. But as we move into the New Story, a new image emerges, the image of the nurturing family model—even the "It takes a village to raise a child" model. You may recall the company towns at the dawn of the industrial revolution. While these were intended to keep the workforce healthy and working hard (i.e., to support profit), they did bring a nurturing family model to work.

But these work models are more than those worn-out labels. Think for a moment of a tight social group you have belonged to. It may have been a Boy or Girl Scout troop, a military platoon, a college athletic team, or a business startup team. As a member, you could always see someone pointing the group in a direction, while someone else was plotting the details of action, and always—there was someone who was cooking up the next new thing to do.

Here's a new way to think of the triad of how people function in organizations. We've renamed the three categories of leaders, organizers, and creative catalysts, as you will see in the following diagram:

What's Your Social Role?

Leaders	Organizers	Creative Catalysts
Sell	Tell	Yell
Set the direction	Plan the details	Create new directions
Take Risks	Minimize risk	Embrace risk
Have vision	Have objectives	Have curiosity
Eye the horizon	Eye the bottom line	Eye inner/outer/white space
Challenge status quo	Accept the status quo	Invent new status quo
Do the right thing	Do the thing right	Do the new thing
Vote with the heart	Vote with the head	Vote with the soul
See an opportunity	See a problem	Create opportunities

What role best suits your gifts? Which role fits best with your purpose, your values, and your story? Given who you are, what are you going to do? You can talk your talk, so what's your walk—your purpose in action?

Putting It All Together

Here are some suggestions for bringing all this together. Create a personal Bring-it-to-Life plan. If you are going to share your gift with others, how will you best do that? Spend some quality time putting together a packet or simple collection of material to craft your story. Besides the obvious business card, there are four other items to craft:

1. **The Purpose Statement**

We call it a structured statement of your purpose. Here is a simplified version:

TO: [Name the ideal change you need to make to live out your purpose.]
IN A WAY THAT: [Name the benefit of this transformation to those you are sharing your value with in living out your purpose.]
SO THAT: [Describe what enables those you interact with to achieve their purposes?]
ALTERNATIVE:
TO: [What is my life purpose? How do I bring it to life? Or, how do I do it better or more often? What changes do I need to make to start living out my purpose?]
IN A WAY THAT: [How do I live out my purpose to share my value, my gift, to positively benefit the people and places who I value and am valued by?]
SO THAT: [How to do it in such a way so that my valued community and I can and do benefit by sharing value and enjoy shared value on purpose?]

In personal branding, the resulting elevator pitch is something like this:
"I am the only person who does this for them in this time, place, and context, and the result/value of that is this."

Now, here's the catch. Absolutely fifty words or less. This is your 30-second TV ad or video.

2. **Storyboard**

A storyboard is "a sequence of drawings, typically with directions and dialogue, representing the shots planned for a movie, video, or TV production." Silicon Valley web developers call this a wireframe.

Remember your story structure? The first part of your story is your purpose. The middle part is about the values you hold sacred and how you know when you are living those out. The last part is about how that all comes together into being.

It's useful to create visual representations (pictures) here. Look at some of the graphics we use. They all came out of our storyboard process.

So, you need at least three pieces. Illustrate how they reinforce each other through an image for your core value and one for your desired role.

3. **Narrative for Action**

About now, you are thinking, "Wow, this sounds like a lot of work." It is. Just walking around with your purpose, values, gift, story, and desired role is a significant step forward. When you are serious about sharing your gift so that you and others can become better together, acting in the here and now is a gift.

Complete an action worksheet. Make it 1 page, less than 200 words. It should cover:

• What is the opportunity? (What are you proposing to do that will make people's lives better or easier?)
• What's the overall strategy (big picture plan) for creating this opportunity?
• What tactics (small-picture actions) will you need to use?
• Logistics and support—what will you need?
• What alliances and partnerships will you need? Who will help you?

4. **The Questions**

Our experience says asking questions is what drives value. You need some questions to ask of others along the way. Here are some topics to start with when you are exploring relationships to give life to your purpose, values, and story:

• *Plan?* What's your intention?
• *Purpose?* What's your gift?
• *Passion?* What gives you joy?

We could add more, but this will get you started. Hint: If you get answers from the Old Story, in the old language—consider whether your purpose includes helping others find the New Story. If not, try to avoid people who will drag you back to the Old Story.

Place is the Next Step Along the Pathway

Our next step concerns place, in both a physical and a metaphorical sense, as in a home or marketplace. Places are locations where interactions occur and things happen, value is exchanged, and people collaborate in forming shared purpose. Our purpose, our story, and all that comes with it are more than neurons firing away in our brains—it all that needs expression to come alive and because we are living, feeling beings that exists in this space, here and now. But, as you will see, a space on its own is not enough—it must become a place.

A village common is more than a few oaks trees and some park benches; it's where people come together in community. A house can be more than a pile of sticks and bricks; it can be a home where family lives and the heart resides.

"Attention. Intention. Action. Insights."

PART I – PURPOSE

Chapter 4: **Do You Live in the Right Place?**

Introduction

Putting purpose in its place for you and me.

Purpose = Lifequest
Place = Living
Practice = Life:
Applying Learnings

As place is to space, unity is to community—
it's the emotional glue that holds it together.

Defining Space and Place

Think about the differences between space and place. A house is just a house—cement, wood, plaster, wiring, plumbing, windows, doors, floors, etc.—nothing else without people. As important as houses and buildings are, they are not nearly as important as people. We have lived in trees, caves, mountaintops, and jungles without real houses. But we cannot live without others, as we are, above all, social beings. A home is the house plus people plus purpose.

So space is important, but place is of utmost importance. We are all related, and relationships are what truly keep us alive. How do we turn space into place? We know that it's important and why it's important, but just as no person is an island, purpose–the sharing of one's gift, and being of service to others–can only happen with and by the grace of others.

Space is physical. Place is metaphysical; it goes beyond the physical into a social dimension. How can we change space into place?

• Re-arrange the furniture in your home (or the first placing of things when you move in). Anyone who has ever walked into a home "staged" for sale gets this. Five to seven seconds (yes, seconds) and the impression is fixed. Often, first impressions are lasting impressions.
• Personalize your workspace. What happens when you are restricted from doing this? There is ample evidence to support the idea that lack of personalization translates into employee disengagement.
• Have conversations with others in a community space such as a political rally in the town square or a farmers' market.

In other words, place is a space in which social interaction occurs and where each person knows that they belong in that place. A place is where space takes on personal meaning. It's about taking meaning from direct and sometimes indirect experiences.

Recently, people who build the spaces we live in have come to realize that the physical characteristics of space do indeed shape our thoughts, emotions, and even our actions. Listen to Winifred Gallagher, author of "The Power of Place":

"The basic principle that links our places and (emotional) states is simple: a good or bad environment promotes good or bad memories, which inspire a good or bad mood, which inclines us toward good or bad behavior. We needn't even be consciously aware of a pleasant or unpleasant environmental stimulus for it to shape our states."

We take meaning from spaces by interacting with others in these spaces, and that meaning is influenced by our ideas, beliefs, and attitudes towards those spaces.

Attitudes + Behavior + Space = Place

You could practice the martial art of Aikido (a behavior) in the middle of a busy intersection (a space) but it wouldn't have the same meaning, purpose or authenticity as doing it in a formal practice space like a dojo (with its expectations of a particular attitude).

Are You in the Right Place?

One of our recurring themes is that if your purpose is not in harmony with what you do at work, then work literally won't work for you. This also holds true for your community—where you live. You experience much stress when there is a barrier to living your purpose and sharing it with others. We've all been there. "This place just doesn't feel right." You feel out of place.

In our consulting practice, the first question that usually comes up after clarifying personal purpose for a client is: "Am I in the right place for that purpose?" It's very predictable that this question arises as you realize that the Old Story is dying and the New Story is growing. And it is greater than the mere physical. We also take meaning from virtual space. In a sense this virtual space has become one of our marketplaces for the value we want to share.

My Place or Ours?

The Old Story is about being physically present in the same place at the same time. We are shifting to a New Story where we don't necessarily have to be in the same space at the same time to collaborate. Technology is bringing us to a point where we can act out the New Story in physical as well as virtual places. A virtual space is a location on the Internet. It opens the gateway to many new opportunities.

Where do you work? The answer to this key question is changing. The Old Story would answer that people needed to be in the same space at the same time in order to work together. And we got very big office buildings. But the New Story does not hold that assumption of the need to be co-located in time and space for collaboration. And we are in transition. For example, at a global level we can be on different continents and only need to connect at the same relative time—think of teleconferences between Los Angeles and New Delhi. Locally, we can dedicate spaces for a team, but not everyone needs to be there at the same time. Currently we have team rooms where people come and go as needed.

Technology is a wonderful connector, provided it can include our need for the comfort of home, a way to light a fire around which we can gather and share life-sustaining stories.

We are only now beginning to explore just what a virtual place is as opposed to a virtual space. In the New Story narrative, it is where social media begins to supplement face-to-face interaction in physical places. Ask yourself these questions to start exploring whether you are in the right place:

• **Live:** What does your neighborhood say about you? In the Old Story world this was all about the status you wanted to broadcast. But that is shifting. Outward status has less social value than it did, and at times can be a liability.

• **Work:** Do you feel comfortable and have a sense of well-being at work? Much research is now being done in this area. After almost two decades of promoting well-being strictly in terms of physical attributes (i.e., weight, blood pressure, diet), we're beginning to define well-being more broadly.

• **Market:** What is your market? The Westernized world is quickly moving toward what some have called a gig economy in which more of us act like micro-businesses in a global marketplace. In our research, our questionnaires are designed in India, administration and data collection happen in the Philippines, and report production is in North Dakota.

> The traditional fixed nature of and the fixation on physical space and place are fixtures of the Old Story—one of ownership, inflexibility, and control. The rapidly changing nature of the virtual world of space and the emerging possibilities of virtual place are part of the New Story—one of co-ownership, fluidity, and collaboration.

Why is Place Important?

If your purpose is your why of whys, then what's the why of place? There is an old saying in architecture: "form follows function." What are the implications if a core function of a space is to communicate something symbolically? What form will that space take? The answer reveals what we call the brand of a place, or place brand.

Signs and symbols give clues to the intended purpose of a place. What gets done here, why it gets done here, and how it connects to some larger life-affirming goodness all emerge through signs and symbols.

Three interrelated things are going on here concerning turning space into place. First, there is the physical, practical part. Place is a crucible for interaction with others. Humans need somewhere to interact. We design and construct places to encourage and support purposeful engagement.

Second, places give you meaning. The German sociologist Georg Simmel said it best in the late 19th century, a high point for the Old Story. He suggested that human society was an intricate web of multiple relations between individuals in constant interaction with one another. These interactions are grounded in time and space—not just some hazy mental activity.

Last, places are important in a symbolic sense. Places are where we can recognize our interconnectedness, our mutuality, and our shared values. They are the where of moving from the me to the we. They are where relatedness and relationships become noticeable. Think of the family holiday dinner; the summer celebrations in the town square or green; the communion of church or temple.

So, the Why of Where and Who is about the larger human community that extends beyond each person. Community lies at the unity—the heart—of how people identify themselves (me/we) and how they interact with one another (space/place).

Brand and Story Sharing

Go back to your story. Are the theme and message of your story reflected in your physical locations? Is your story consistent with the virtual spaces, and the social networks, you operate within?

It is not unusual in today's world that people physically locate themselves close to people with shared values. A politically progressive person in the current United States will likely move away from a politically conservative environment, for example. And the other way round. People discover that if they are dedicated to their purpose, they need to live where their brand is celebrated, not just tolerated—thus red and blue states have evolved.

Place is the stage on which you play out your purpose story. It must be the right setting or your message will get lost in the background noise. The change from the Old into the New, the move from this into that, has become a conscious choice, particularly in regards to place.

We admire a Zen philosophy that focuses on being and doing—based on what one values—at work, at play, and in life. This alignment, through mindfulness, helps people be more engaged with others and their communities, and increases the satisfaction they derive from that.

We began with purpose because that captures the larger philosophy of matching what one does for a livelihood with one's life quest to answer the questions Why am I here? And Why are we here? In today's world, this seems to be increasing in importance because of a shift in attitudes about work and life in general. We are quickly moving from the Old Story of Profit to the New Story of Purpose as the main reason why people behave in a certain way socially. In this transition, fear turns to love, space to place, house to home, and scarcity to abundance. Melody Beattie says:

"Gratitude unlocks the fullness of life. It can turn a meal into a feast, a house into a home, a stranger into a friend."

It is in community where human beings find and share their value, their gifts, and ways they can be in service to others. These things do not—and cannot—exist in a vacuum. We are relational beings. In the Old Story of Profit, people were often seen as mere instruments of capitalism—as units of production.

In the New World of Purpose, of People, and Planet, shared purpose and sharing value are important to the individual, but even more to the community—the exchanging, the sharing, the giving of our gifts and company, our wit and humor, our kindness and caring, our laughter and sorrow, our presence and being there—these interactions are what make us truly human and rich beyond belief.

This implies that the experience of place needs to reflect and reinforce those shared values if we are to move forward, to design and construct a future in which becoming better together is what gets us out of bed in the morning.

Shifting Gears

The next chapter shifts the social context of our writing. We start moving from the me to the we. You've gotten a little taste of this shift here, but we now dive deeper. This change in emphasis is only one part of the larger narrative of moving from the Old Story of Profit First—where profits come first, not people—to a more communal striving for a happier, healthier people and planet, putting profit in its proper place, a supporting role to promote health and happiness for all.

"Place is where the heart is."

PART II – PLACE

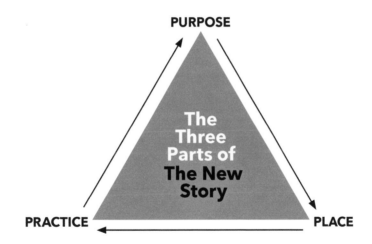

PURPOSE

The
Three
Parts of
**The New
Story**

PRACTICE

PLACE

Chapter 5: Will Your City Be DOA* in the 21st Century?

G/host Town U.S.A.?

Do you remember seeing photographs of or visiting old ghost towns across the United States, particularly in the west? Soon, we'll be seeing new ghost towns across the country. Will your local government be one of them? It could be, but needn't be. There are plenty of problems ahead for sure, but there are possibilities for renewal as well.

We've been exploring a number of potential scenarios for local governments—small cities, towns, and counties—and have concluded that in some of them, local governments will cease to exist in the next two decades. So, why should you care? You should care if you don't want to leave behind a legacy of dying and dead cities and counties.

The purpose of this section is to give you a realistic picture of what is about to happen in many American local governments and abroad, and insight into what you need to do, now, to prepare for that. First, let's look at what we can reasonably expect to happen that will affect your sustainability—after all, you'll want to thrive, not just survive.

*Dead On Arrival

We've found four things that put many cities at risk:

1. *Significant reduction in direct and indirect revenues within five years.*
Larger government entities are going broke, either through deliberate revenue reductions or bad investment decisions such as retirement funds and complex hybrid investments. Local governments can't rely on stable revenue transfers from regional, state, and national resources any longer. All indications are that this trend will continue.

2. *Talent migration to larger metro areas.*
Talent, the social capital that starts and grows commerce, is migrating away from rural and suburban areas to large metroplexes that offer a wider variety of experiences, opportunities, and services. There is a scaling factor here, in that you have to be of a certain population size—let's say 250,000—to offer a quality of life essential for the Old Story. Metro areas are heterogeneous, which means you are likely to be around people who don't share your purpose.

3. *Resource constraints* (i.e. water, energy, and transportation).
Water is getting harder to manage in the western United States. Much of the United States has reached a resource limit to growth. We must reduce consumption to survive. We must replace carbon energy. Our national transportation infrastructure, including air travel, is outdated and crumbling.

4. *Aging in place.*
Our populations are getting older and demanding more services, especially health-care. The young and well off leave their communities of origin behind with smaller tax bases and gravitate to the growing megacities. They leave behind the old, poor, and less able, vastly increasing the strain on provision of local social services and healthcare.

Why Is This Happening?

Local governments are now caught up in a global web of systems—social, technical, commercial, and governmental. What is happening at a global scale impacts the local more profoundly and quickly than in the past:

- Increasing diversity of demographics, belief systems, and cultural heritage
- Complexity as everything and everyone gets connected to everything else
- Personal awareness of global events through social media
- Speed of change and word of mouth
- Volatility, uncertainty, and lack of trust in environments, economic, and political institutions
- Increasing self-knowledge, particularly among youth, which causes a shift in desires, expectations, and demands

What Can I Do About It?

What do you as a civic leader need to do to ensure your community adapts to this changing world? First, have a strategy—one with several contingencies to guide your responses to these impending forces. Without a strategy, you'll be at the mercy of all these things outside your direct control. You'll face more competition, more complexity, more choice, less control, and less clarity of outcomes.

Instead, develop the capability to forecast, anticipate, and change before you are faced with a certain demise. What are your first steps? What do you need to do today in order to achieve your vision of the future?

The first, and usually the hardest, thing to do is to honestly understand and clearly articulate the original purpose of your city. Why is it there? Historic accident? Product of a bygone economic era? Now look to today. Why do your citizens call this place their home? Why not be elsewhere?

Your personal purpose is your True North: your guiding star. If you know why you exist—what your purpose is—then you can make all your decisions guided by that purpose, which you share clearly with all of your stakeholders. This is as true for the cities we inhabit as it is for each of us. You are looking for the True North, the guiding star, for your city.

Next, you need a brand, and not just some trite slogan like "Everybody's Hometown." What is unique, valuable, and defensible about your city?

Now determine your branding strategy. You know your city's purpose, and have a solid brand, but how do you communicate that to a larger community? How do you transform your community into one that attracts positive word-of-mouth, talent, commerce, and capital?

Once you've created and successfully launched your brand's strategy, everyone touched by your brand enjoys the bond of a shared purpose. Shared purpose creates the loyalty and relevance that your civic brand richly deserves.

In this digital era of transparency, it is crucial to listen to and connect with your stakeholders to strengthen their loyalty and trust, internally and externally, to build long-term relationships. That only comes by engaging your brand with all your stakeholders to co-create enduring win-win relationships.

If you have a job that lets you influence the strategic direction of your community (whether through your paid employment or a volunteer role in your community), get up tomorrow and start thinking, planning, and working on three initiatives:

1. Put someone in charge of strategic planning, branding, and innovation.
2. Develop a plan for consolidation of services as revenues collapse.
3. Make continuous civic sustainability and well-being your central policy goal.

What do you get with all this? You get a city that attracts all the resources it needs. You get a city that is more concerned with quality of life than size. You get a happy place to live, work, and learn—the brand you own is the brand you earn.

PART II – PLACE

Chapter 6: How to Keep It from Happening to You/r City?

Our original op-ed blogs on the major challenges facing local governments in the early 21st century generated much feedback. Folks have asked us to expand on how to keep these oncoming forces of change at bay. You can make these forces work for you—not against you—if you have a strategy. Our intent is to help you craft that strategy.

Now let's drill down on a couple of major issues to point the way towards a sustainable pathway for civic development. First, we want to explore civic engagement and life satisfaction as overarching public goals, and then link that to the development of your city's brand.

As we shift to a post-industrial, post-capitalist society, there is perhaps no better venue than community to express having well-being as the primary motivating public policy goal.

Happy or Crappy?
There are many definitions of well-being. For example, Bhutan and Denmark use Gross National Happiness indices instead of GNP for planning and evaluation. We

recommend looking at this complex topic through the lens of a balanced score-card. Taken from the Old Story, a balanced scorecard is simply a multiple input way of measuring performance. For example, a balanced scorecard for a student would be the grades from all their classes, not just one class. When we translate this idea into a vocabulary for the New Story we get a model balanced scorecard, with five major elements. Start with these indices of health, place, community, learning, and economic opportunity:

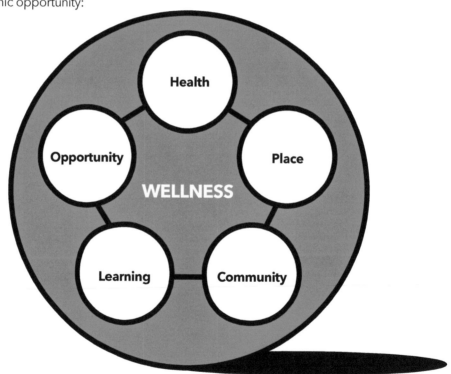

- **Community:** Amount of local social capital and the strength of social networks.

- **Place:** Physical, social, environmental, and economic characteristics of an area, which shape our thoughts, emotions, and actions.

- **Learning:** Educational resources and opportunities in an area.

- **Health:** State of physical, psychological, and spiritual health in an area.

- **Economic Opportunity:** Diversity of structure, upward mobility pathways, and a future-oriented economic development plan and practice.

Going To The Well

Although many Smart City initiatives measure well-being around rich quantitative data, well-being is a powerful qualitative measure that resonates with people. Different cities weigh these five defining factors differently, usually playing to an existing strength or historic factor.

Going forward, cities need to balance these factors, neglecting none. We find a great emphasis on place in our current research, an emphasis that appears as a need for safety and security. This is where people start. It is certainly a necessity, but the cities with the highest well-being go well beyond that, for example, serenity.

North Star

There are, as we have found, two other requirements to make well-being-as-a-goal a viable method of governance. First, make sure your leadership is committed to making your civic core purpose—Why do we exist?—into your North Star, a compass to guide everything you do. When changes are being weighed, measure them against this North Star to see whether they are a good fit. We see a valuable opportunity here to develop a reliable process to guide all legislative initiatives and citizen evaluation of government officials' and agencies' performance in office.

Second, implement an audit process that reliably assesses progress towards well-being and balanced scorecard goals. No fudging allowed—the audit process needs to be transparent even to the extent that it is managed by an outside party, such as a citizens' oversight board.

Giving Voice to Vision

To sum up, adopting well-being as a community performance goal is key to ensuring your community isn't Dead on Arrival in 2020 and beyond. It is not simply about the number of things you do. It's also about the vision and process through which all your stakeholders work together collaboratively based on a shared positive purpose—a sustainable win-win relationship—with clear plans and goals at all levels. *How do you fold community well-being into your brand strategy?* We have some solid ideas for you.

"Historians look back, futurists ahead, but today is all that exists."

PART II – PLACE

Chapter 7: **So, What's Your Community Brand?**

Once you have the civic well-being angle covered, you communicate it through branding.

What is a Brand?

A brand is a living, breathing relationship between you and your stakeholders. The focus of that relationship becomes the core of your civic brand, a clearly defined entity with an associated promise of value, purpose, and values.

It's important to note that a brand is what "they," your stakeholders, say it is—which is not always the same as what you say it is. A brand is the sum of all that you do and don't do as experienced and interpreted by others. In the case of a community place, the brand is the shared experience of the place you are stewards of and the people who congregate there.

If you don't have a positive purpose and share it, you won't have a positive shared experience. Word of mouth picks up velocity through social media, interconnected-ness, and the global village, as well as through peer-to-peer review sites, and smart phone apps. Today is a new era of transparency, authenticity, and the never-ending thirst for trust. If citizens and other important stakeholders such as employers and investors don't trust you to maintain and grow their brand experience in a positive, shared way, you'll lose.

Listen to the Leaders

Alison Maxwell, deputy director of economic development for Glendale, California, says:

"A city is not Coca-Cola—it's a living, breathing, amorphous entity. Good branding can bring the sum of the parts together and give you a hook to hang your identity on."

Place Brand

A place brand is the combination of the specific purpose, values, and value associated with a defined place and mental space, be it a city, town, or county. Make sure your local government is a well-recognized brand that is easy to identify and relate to. If your stakeholders can't quickly feel and share the uniqueness and value of your brand, then you're indistinguishable at best or memorable for all the wrong reasons at worst.

When that happens, your stakeholders abandon you and your word of mouth only gets worse. Your savvier competitors—and they are many—will be working day and night to build their brand at your expense. Thus, you will lose the competition for the hearts, minds, wallets, and feet of your stakeholders and you will become a collection of crumbling, half-forgotten buildings—in other words, a modern-day ghost town—and you'll be out of a job to boot.

Place branding is about much more than geographic location. It's a social space. Show and share your distinctness in easy-to-understand, concrete terms, and values that will appeal to your stakeholders' hearts and heads—showing that you care.

Building a Powerful Civic Brand

Talent is the engine of the innovation economy. Brand is the emotional link that connects these bright people to your place. The more talented and well-educated folks are, the more choices they have. If they choose your approach to governance, then you'll attract and retain the best and the brightest, and the tax base, jobs, economic resiliency, favorable word-of-mouth they bring.

So, what to do? Look at where your community came from, where you are today, and where you should and could go in the future. Then start working backwards from your ideal trajectory point guided by the North Star of your core purpose to start figuring out how to get from where you are today to where you want to be as a civic brand:

- **Step #1** Define what today is your civic brand in the hearts and minds of your stakeholders.
- **Step #2** Do a gap analysis of the difference of what you think your brand is and what it is thought of by others.
- **Step #3** Determine what to start doing, what to do more of, and what to stop doing.
- **Step #4** Develop a plan of action to clarify, deepen, and sweeten your relationship with your stakeholders.
- **Step #5** Put that plan into action as soon as possible—in as many ways possible—and track the results, making course adjustments along the way.
- **Step #6** Communicate what you're doing, inviting people to participate through town halls, interviews, community events, social media, county fairs, etc., while always asking: What do we want to be remembered for, and are we acting on that? Work with the community to make sure your brand promise consistently delivers value.

Think of water out West, an irreplaceable, life-sustaining resource. Then think of trying to live without it. A city without a positive brand is in similar danger. You have to replenish the wells of brand goodwill on an ongoing basis, or your community will run dry.

More and more local governments are hiring Chief Innovation Officers, which is a positive step forward. But the Innovation Officer will only be a source of short-term novelty value if it is not made part of something much bigger and more permanent.

Innovation, like good service, must be a cultural trait, imbued, recognized, and rewarded across the entire bureaucracy of local government.

How Do You Get the Word Out?

Communicate by first tracking, measuring, analyzing, extrapolating, and predicting. Use ROI studies and invest in the most promising, biggest-return communications. Communicate from peer-to-peer, to one-to-many, to many-to-many, 24/7/365. Don't shotgun it. Define your stakeholders, identify the best channels to engage them, and frame your message in their terms—not yours—to start an ongoing conversation.

Use an interactive multi-media approach including social media. To start, define your lowest hanging fruit and be quick to demonstrate action and seriousness. Everyone is in the marketing department, whether that's their official job or not. All local government employees, contractors, and volunteers define your community's brand to one another and to those beyond, both in what they say and in how they act.

To assess whether your strategy is working, set up a multi-indicator dashboard (quantitative and qualitative) and do routine audits of external sources. Track brands by setting up a baseline of key emotional indicators with pools of corresponding people and then track sentiment over time. Now, let's explore the nuts and bolts of how to move your city in this well-being, well-branded direction.

"The future is here; it's just not evenly distributed."

PART II — PLACE

Chapter 8: **How to Move Your City Forward**

In the previous chapters, we outlined some driving forces of change, reviewed aspects of civic well-being, and brought it together under the umbrella of place branding. We suggested three major steps:

1. Put someone in charge of strategic planning, branding, and innovation.
2. Develop a plan for consolidation of services as revenues collapse.
3. Make continuous sustainability your central policy goal.

We're going to talk here about each of these in more detail. But we're also going to add a fourth step:

4. Create an Audit and Response System so you'll be able to document and leverage the results of your efforts.

Put Someone in Charge

Any city has many stakeholders, and often they are in competition with one another for resources and policy priorities. It takes a strong leader to bring these factions together and focus on the good of the whole—on a purpose larger than themselves.

We have found a great way to start this process is by using a process called The Delphi Technique. It assembles, in an anonymous fashion, a large group of civic leaders to identify policy priorities and rank them in terms of impact and priority for action. Out of that process comes consensus on which direction to move and what will have the most effect in terms of well-being and branding. A volunteer subset of this panel then becomes the group keeping the planning, branding, and innovation process alive.

Develop a Plan

This is a straightforward strategic planning exercise. Often, cities don't have people experienced in this process—or with the skills to evaluate competitive players, systemic weaknesses, long time frames, and a regional approach. This may be where you want to involve outside resources to help. There are two that we recommend you start a conversation with:

• International City Management Association (ICMA): This is the premier forum for community leaders and has a very extensive network of professionals.
• Alliance for Innovation: This organization exists to help communities innovate, stay future-focused, and share learnings across local boundaries.

Central Policy Goal: Sustainability

Many leaders don't know how to define this in operational terms, i.e., in terms of things that can be reliably observed and measured. A good place to start is by do-ing a review of current efforts underway in other communities to learn from others what your policy implementation metrics need to be.

Given the ever-larger role technology is playing in today's world, a good place to start your search is to assess your community's readiness to leverage technology as a basis of promoting sustainability. There has been much effort on this over the past two decades and readiness assessment is now a mature process.

Now, we come to our last recommendation for moving forward.

Audit the Process

You would not want to fly in a plane without a compass, altitude indicator or air-speed instrument. So don't risk the future of your community on efforts that aren't guided, over time, by valid and reliable metrics.

Every community is different and has its own brand. You need an audit process that fits your individual situation. Private companies have dealt with this issue for quite a while, and have found that using a number of factors and numerous indicators for each factor is the most effective approach.

This process is called a community Balanced Scorecard, which we have detailed above. Create a balanced scorecard in your community, under the direction of the team that grows out of the Delphi Technique.

In today's age of government transparency, the system needs to have an interface that is open to the public, but a database behind it that is not subject to tampering, modification or manipulation. That interface is a "dashboard," composed of a dynamic set of indicators keyed to your situation.

In conclusion, we hope you have found these few chapters to be inspiring and valuable. These ideas are by no means the final answer to keeping your city from becoming DOA in the 21st Century. But they're a sound start—provided they are put into practice.

From U.S.
to US.

PART II – PLACE

Chapter 9: **Putting Your Place Brand on the Map**

We've been exploring branding as a strategy for sustainability and thrive-ability for local governments. We keep getting questions about this, questions like Why is branding, and specifically place branding, so important? What is it? How do you start the process? Here we unpack that idea.

Why is Place Branding So Important?
Branding is important because your town is in competition with other local governments for highly talented and resourceful residents, businesses, and organizations. The key to sustainable economic development is becoming human talent that resides in communities. These are people—"that creative class of people" as Richard Florida has called them—to come live, stay, and grow their families and businesses in your town. Branding is the emotional magnet that will draw them to you, and keep them there.

What is Place Branding?
A brand is a living, breathing relationship between your stakeholders and your civic brand. The civic brand is a clearly defined and identified entity with an associated promise of value, purpose, and values.

Who Defines Your Place Brand?

A brand is what your stakeholders say it is—not what you say it is. A brand is the sum of all that you do and don't do as experienced and interpreted by others. In the case of a place brand, it is the shared experience of the place you are stewards of and the people who congregate there.

Space + Place

Space is the physical areas of your community—for example, open areas, great recreational facilities, clean air and water, and climate. Place is also the social aspect of who you are in your community, and what those Places represent to members of the community. Think of a personal brand. The ideal American male is described as "tall, handsome, and athletic." OK, that's the physical brand part. But that person could also be described as "warm, funny, outgoing, and compassionate." That's the social brand part.

So, a community's Place Brand is about the unique core purpose, values, and value of a place for stakeholders.

Your Core Purpose is Your True North: Your Guiding Star

If you know why you exist—your purpose—then your Place Brand can make all your decisions guided by that purpose, which you can then share with all of your stakeholders.

114

Places compete with other places for people, resources, and businesses. Global competition for cities consists of 3 million small cities/towns, 3,000 large cities, and 500 metropolises in an era of rapid change, 24/7 social media, and ever increasing transparency.

The purpose of Place Branding is to turn a place from a location into a destination—a place where people want to invest, live, work, and visit. The process of targeting stakeholders' hearts, minds, feet, and wallets is based on the visual, verbal, and visceral expression of a place. This consists of the aims, communications, and general culture of the place's stakeholders and the overall place design, with the goal of favorably impacting the perceptions of a place, and positioning it in the minds of its stakeholders and supporters.

The purpose of Place Branding is to create a singular brand for the place and to encompass it in all its offerings and interactions. This creates a unique picture of the place at every level of interaction from the stakeholder point of view. This also helps in removing the need to present a case-by-case picture of the place for each of its offerings to stakeholders.

Ultimately, a Place Brand is the promise of value—a promise you must keep. Effective branding can assist in making a place desirable. Successful Place Brands market their unique history, geography, lifestyle, culture, diversity, and economy.

How Do You Start?

Place Branding is a complex process, due to the diversity of stakeholders involved in the process. In general, derive a Place Brand from existing assets of the place such as its value offering or public perception. Alternately, derive the Place Brand from created assets such as events, policies, and abstract concepts such as tolerance. We usually engage in Place Branding with a four-step exploration. But first we start with a Place Brand strategic map, and then engage in a four-step process to build a Place Brand:

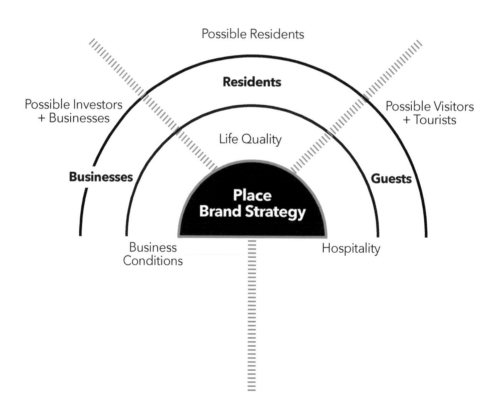

1. **Brand Mapping:** Identify and recruit a small team of community leaders to work with. This is usually seven to twelve people who will commit the time to work with you both on-site and remotely.

2. **Brand Audit:** Define your local government brand in the hearts and minds of your stakeholders today. What does the Chamber of Commerce advertise? If you did a focus group with a cross section of community leaders, what would they say? What would they put on the back of a T-shirt?

3. **Brand Analysis:** Do a gap analysis of the difference between what you think your brand is and what it actually is, by asking outsiders. This is where you can leverage the value of impartial outside observers. You say one thing, but I see another. How do others see it?

4. **Brand Articulation:** Determine what to start doing, what to do more of, and what to stop doing. We use a unique method to identify the best places for you to devote your energies.

Next Steps for You

Once you've completed these steps, you have a decision to make. Do you want to move forward and execute a Place Brand strategy? Will it be a priority? How will you manage that process? These are all-important questions you need to answer from business and community perspectives.

"To live only for some future goal is shallow."

PART III – PRACTICE AND WORK

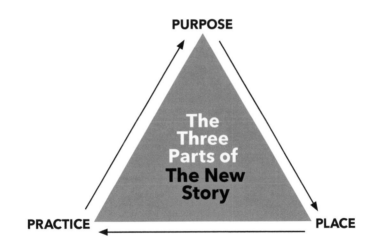

PURPOSE

The
Three
Parts of
The New
Story

PRACTICE

PLACE

119

Chapter 10: Reimagining the Context of Work—Why Purpose?

Purpose is also known as "Your reason for getting up in the morning."
~ Bryan Dik Ph.D.

Work Isn't Working Anymore

We live in an increasingly purposeless world filled with purposeless work. The Old Story and its attendant social institutions were designed to promote continuous growth, first through extraction of non-renewable resources, later by industrial efficiency, and now through manipulation of financial systems—and always through cronyism. As we have mentioned before, the Old Story institutions are no longer supportive of personal well-being (integration of body, mind, and spirit), let alone human wholeness (integration of individuals into a greater whole). Work is a central human activity that provides sustenance, community, meaning, identity, well-being, and wholeness.

Shared purpose is the social-psychological glue that binds humans together. It includes a commonly held belief system, which informs our attitudes and ultimately our behavior. Why is purpose important now? Purpose is important because humankind has reached a point in its evolution where it can consciously choose its guiding principle: creation or destruction.

Purpose: Find Your Why—**Your Guiding North Star**

Why Purpose?

Purpose is the Why of our Whys. All humans are in and on a purpose quest, whether they know it or not. The sole purpose of human existence is ultimately our soul purpose, which raises the questions:

- **Why are we here?**
- **What are we to do?**

We are here to find our purpose and the corresponding path to its fulfillment so that we may become better together. Life is about what we are becoming. It is about turning this into that, and what matters most is not the this or the that, but:

- the into, the transition, because shift happens constantly,
- the emotional experience of transformation through creation, recreation, and conflict co-resolution, and
- the movement from fear to love, from me to we, and from anger and angst to amity and abundance.

Why Now?

The New Story of Work needs to be started to take the place of the Old Story, and shared for the salvation of our souls, livelihoods, and planet. The Old Story of Why are we here? (endless expansion) and What are we to do? (exploit the planet and each other) is a huge dying liability, and has no replacement. We are in dire need of the New Story of how to get out of this big fat mess we are mired in, and to start on the path to transformation so we may become better together through individual and shared positive purpose, and an awakening to our shared wholeness and inescapable mutuality.

The power of the old myths—sold to the masses and perpetuated by America's rich powerful elite (the one percent) for generations—is dying.

The Old Story was built on top of a number of other myths such as Manifest Destiny, Westward Ho!, the Rugged Frontiersman, the Lone Cowboy, the Self-Made Man, and the American Dream. From 1950 to 1975 this dream became a reality for more than not as the postwar boom, based on American global supremacy, provided a rising tide that lifted many boats.

By 1980, the 1950s myths of Infinite Growth, Everybody Can Become Middle Class, and The Business of America is Business, collectively known as the American Dream, turned into the American Nightmare on Main Street. These myths have not been replaced, so we are operating in a vacuum without a compass.

We need to give birth to a new philosophy constructed upon shared positive purpose, values, and value; rethinking profit, people, planet; and creating a new pathway to creating a new socially forward story: planet, people, profit.

Why Work? And What's the Purpose of Work?

Some have asked us: Why focus on work? Because the very nature of work as we have known it for several hundred years is changing, and that is driving other profound changes in the rest of our lives.

What do we hope to accomplish with our perspective on the New Story of Work? Bottom line, we seek to:

• Awaken concerned people to their need to re/discover their Purpose, Place, and Practice for sharing that purpose.
• Provide them with a pathway for discovering their purpose, particularly in the workplace.
• Address how civic leaders and others can create community purpose.

The workplace is where so many people spend so much time doing things they really don't like and don't want to. They often don't understand the purpose—the why—of what they're asked, directed and forced into doing. They work hard and achieve little, or hardly work, leaving them with no or little sense of purpose.

Inner and Outer Wealth

Many people are in denial that the crumbling of our society, as we know, it has begun. But you don't have to look much further than the news media to find stark evidence of this happening. The New York Times recently reported:

"Suicide in the United States has surged to the highest levels in nearly 30 years, a federal data analysis has found, with increases in every age group except older adults. The rise was particularly steep for women. It was also substantial among middle-aged Americans, sending a signal of deep anguish from a group whose suicide rates had been stable or falling since the 1950s."

Why is this happening? The reasons are many and complex. We surmise that more and more people are unemployed, underemployed, or misemployed, which means they don't have a life, and either no living or a poor living at that. The flat or declining incomes, assets, and percentage of overall wealth of the ninety-nine percent for the past three decades reinforces this view.

The same type of thing happened at the beginning of the Industrial Revolution. Emile Durkheim, one of the founders of the modern academic discipline we call sociology, concluded that there was no sense of purpose or of belonging then. And we conclude similarly today.

It is our contention that a sense of belonging is built on a sense of connection to others through shared, life-affirming purpose greater than any one of us. Bringing purpose to work and then putting it to work is enormously important.

Putting Personal Purpose to Work

Purpose is like oxygen for the soul. Our sole purpose is to provide an outlet for the soul through finding and then following a purposeful path to healthy profits, yes, but also to a healthy planet and people. This is made increasingly evident by the shifting focus from shareholders to stakeholders. If life ceases to be sustainable on our small planet, there will be no customers, clients or corporations—forever.

Purposeless work ("I'm only here for the bucks.") has a profound and often devastating impact on workers, their families, their communities, and the planet. That's why we have chosen to focus on work. It is a common social activity which gives us meaning, without which we are lost.

Backstory: What We Are Building On

Our culture is built on—informed and influenced by—a triadic tradition, pervading cultures east and west, old and new. Triadic relationships, relational groupings of three, are important, universal relational building blocks. Examples of triadic relationships include: profit, breaking even, and loss; body, mind, and soul; mother, father, and child; Father, Son and Holy Ghost; before, now, and after; left, middle, and right, etc.

All things are relative (they only exist in relation to something else; no big without small and medium) and cannot exist in our minds without relativity. Most concepts only come alive with an opposite and a transitional being or state. Most things in life are not black or white, but are grey—part of a spectrum. The purpose triad is below:

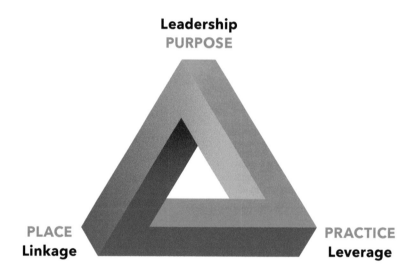

Leadership
PURPOSE

PLACE
Linkage

PRACTICE
Leverage

How Do These Three Parts Fit Together?

Our core purpose is to guide people, teams, organizations, and communities to awaken to their potential of wholeness in life and put it to work—to have a renewing sense of purpose, of mattering, and being a part of something much greater. Wholeness, in the sense that we intend it, is a bringing together our unified selves (body, mind, and spirit) into a great whole guided by the North Star of shared purpose.

"The future depends on the beauty of your dream."

PART III – PRACTICE AND WORK

Chapter 11: **Leading with Purpose**

"Leadership is unlocking people's potential to become better."
~ Bill Bradley

"Purpose without leadership is like a fish on a bicycle."
~ Whitney Vosburgh

"Leadership without purpose is just management." ~ Charlie Grantham

This portion of our journey addresses two interrelationships. First, there is the continuum that grows from identifying what your purpose is to determining where that is lived out, and ultimately what you do to manifest purpose at work and in life. The other factor can be thought of as what your relative social position is in work organizations. There are many definitions of this organizational role. We are simplifying those dimensions to three categories: leadership, management, and creative catalysts of change—a new category that we think plays the protagonist in the New Story of Work. In essence, these catalysts are those in our society who continuously practice creativity and invention.

It is not our aim here to engage in a definitive discussion of organizational struc-tures. Our goal is to give you some conceptual tools to reimagine the context in which these roles bring purpose to life and to work. To be clear, let's go back to our illustration of differences between leaders, organizers, and creative catalysts.

What's Your Social Role?

Leaders	Organizers	Creative Catalysts
Sell	Tell	Yell
Set the direction	Plan the details	Create new directions
Take Risks	Minimize risk	Embrace risk
Have vision	Have objectives	Have curiosity
Eye the horizon	Eye the bottom line	Eye inner/outer/white space
Challenge status quo	Accept the status quo	Invent new status quo
Do the right thing	Do the thing right	Do the new thing
Vote with the heart	Vote with the head	Vote with the soul
See an opportunity	See a problem	Create opportunities

This section focuses on Leadership, so let's unpack our definitions for the first row of boxes. Purpose is the reason you are on this planet now. It exists to guide you by answering your existential question: Why? The purpose of leadership is to create a shared positive purpose as a motivating force to transform the present into a desired shared future state. Much is written about innovation and, to a lesser degree, transformation, but both are often misunderstood. Innovation is the act of creation done to stay in place, today. Whereas transformation is the act of creation done to stay ahead tomorrow—and long into the future. And everyone has a role to play in both innovation and transformation.

Leaders point the direction, and managers figure out how to get there. Managers live in the present, operate by the rules, and manage the culture. They see that things are done right. These are the folks who make sure the railroad runs on time and stays on the tracks already laid down by their leaders.

Creative catalysts—creative catalysts of change—are often overlooked in the life of organizations. Creative catalysts create purpose and constantly renew their sense of purpose—they continually invent and reinvent themselves, their work, and world. But they can create tremendous tension. They are the grain of sand in the oyster that builds the pearl.

Now, let us expand the basic idea that personal purpose manifests in different forms dependent upon the social role you play at work. Keep this 3X3 table in mind; we will continue to come back to it over and over:

(3x3)	Leadership	Management	Creative Catalysts
Purpose	?	?	?
Place	?	?	?
Practice	?	?	?

Take Me To Your Leader

If the purpose of leadership is to create shared purpose, how is that lived out every day at work?

It's our observation that many people who hold leadership roles really behave more like managers. That is, these folks have objectives, not vision; and they minimize risk instead of taking risks like genuine leaders do. So, to be clear, let's start with an agreed upon definition of leadership and management:

• Leaders move people in the direction of a vision of a desired shared future.
• Managers control people and processes in the direction of previously agreed on goals.

While we need both leadership and management and, part of the problem today is that most organizations are not led by purposeful leaders.

According to Ross Ashcroft, Co-founder of Renegade, Inc.:

"The world is currently over-managed and under-led."

An organization's success is dependent upon true leadership, not just efficient management. The emerging workplace is more uncertain; change has sped up; and customers have become notoriously fickle because they have frictionless access to a wealth of shared information, reviews, and ratings.

This increased volatility requires companies to become more agile in running their entire business enterprise. This in turn necessitates leadership that can change direction and operations quicker than the competition, management that is just as agile, and creative catalysts that stay well ahead of the curve.

Leadership isn't for everyone. Some people are content just doing things, not wondering about the why.

When Charlie was in the army, his boss had to write an Officer Efficiency Report every year. The classic line was, "This officer is destined to go through life pushing on doors marked pull." Can you imagine the image this brought up when you were being considered for a leadership position? Do you want a manager who is always pushing against the tide, or a leader who is taking charge and pulling your business into the future?

And then there would be the independent who keeps asking, "What's the purpose of the door? And how about this new, better door?"

A focus of this book is the need for a New Story of Work. In terms of leadership this is the key distinction: the Old Story was always about pushing forward, overcoming resistance, being aggressive, moving into the future. The New Story, which is only now emerging, is more about pulling the future toward you, surrounding it, encircling it, and in forming it. The Old Story is a divisive framework; the New Story is an inclusive framework.

How Do You Do It?

We believe making the Brand New Purpose of Work a reality requires recruiting talent with high leadership potential to begin with. Then smart organizations need to put in place a well-supported leadership development program. And these programs should have several integrated components.

We'd like to note that this type of leadership development used to be commonplace in large companies through the 80s but has since largely disappeared, driven by the false lure of quarterly results and faster turnover of senior management—again the Old Story of Work in operation.

First, sort out high-potential folks from those who won't be leaders. The answer is easy; execution difficult. Look for people who have already demonstrated leadership or impressive individual initiative. For example, in the public sector consider people with a background in the Peace Corps and, more recently, AmeriCorps. In the private sector, look for involvement in things like code camps, hackathons, and formal entrepreneurial training programs like GirlMade. These are the people who always seem to step up and volunteer to lead new efforts, from product launches to the summer office picnic.

Second, another component of an effective leadership development program is to create a pathway to increasingly responsible jobs. Related to this is giving heightened visibility to high performers so you can ensure continuity of leadership. Done right, there will always be a pool of people to choose from when senior leadership vacancies occur. Everyone always knows who should be placed in that next critical opening.

Third, have formal individual mentoring and sponsoring programs where one-on-one relationships are developed. We can all remember that one teacher, that one coach, that one professor, that one senior person who made all the difference in helping us develop our direction. Asking leadership candidates to recall their experiences with mentors and sponsors can help you find people who have had prior positive leadership development experiences. And good past experiences can help inspire and guide future development actions.

Back to the Future: Purpose as a Guiding North Star

A core action for future leaders will be leading the process of transformation, which is applied creativity that makes a long-term positive difference guided by a vision of shared purpose. A key task, then, for true leaders, is to guide others towards this purposeful transformation—to turn vision into action.

Lastly, the purposeful workplace will be looking for people who are actively engaged in self-leadership or strategic personal development—constant discovery and rediscovery of purpose. This is an evolving skill set. In the new world of work, people won't be able to depend on folks down the hall in Human Resources to assist them with their leadership development.

"The future belongs to those who change it"

PART III – PRACTICE AND WORK

Chapter 12: Where Purpose gets Connected and Put into Place–Place Linkage

In the previous section, we talked about how creative catalysts create purpose, leaders express purpose, and managers make it real. We switch gears a bit here and focus on how that purpose, and ultimately shared purpose, gets expressed in physical and virtual environments. If the previous section could be called the what, this one is the where.

Space + Brand = Place

But how do these ideas get linked together? When you enter a place (be it a work place or a community place) the organizational brand message is instantaneously broadcast. And that's why we see place is such an important expression of brand purpose. Just like the old saying, "You don't get a second chance to make a first impression," a brand-new impression is very hard to change. There is strong linkage between brand and culture:

Shared Purpose
by all stakeholders

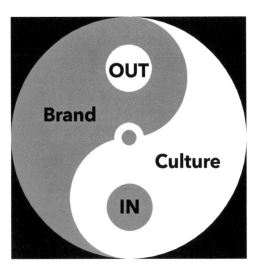

• Brand is culture inside out and culture is brand outside in—the two can't be separated.

• Space is where the culture is housed physically but place is where the brand/culture is housed emotionally and intellectually—in all stakeholders inside and out the space.

Space vs. Place

Space is a physical concept devoid of meaning. Humans add meaning to space and it becomes place. To put it simply, space is like a house, and place is like a home. It's beyond this section to explain the social psychology of that except to say it's an established theory that people develop a sense of social meaning from the interactions they have with one another and with spaces. For example, walking through a zoo imparts a certain sense of wonder and gives a particular meaning to the animal kingdom. Traveling on safari through a jungle gives an almost entirely different meaning to the same phenomenon.

Two of our favorite authors on this topic are cultural geographers Yi-Fu Tuan and Edward Relph. They see two major avenues towards deriving meaning from space. First, a direct one through our senses (i.e. vision, smell, and hearing). Second, through indirect, conceptual means such as symbols, myths, and rituals of use. Think, for example, of the liturgy of Christian worship, which is a fixed set of ceremonies and words. The place of networks, tribes, and communities: where *me* becomes *we*.

To offer a slightly different viewpoint on space and place, we suggest that the blending of pure physical space into a more social place is where the transition from the me to the we occurs. It's where purpose becomes shared purpose.

Community, for us, lies at the unity of how people identify themselves (me/we) with how they interact with one another. Exactly how does the me become we?

All the World's a Stage

Shared purpose gets acted out on that stage, be it a workplace or a community place. As the Old Story begins to fade and wither away, a New Story is being created. But, if you observe closely, the stage upon which that gets acted out is also changing.

It used to be that if you said space/place a mental image of a physical location leapt to mind. Architects saw walls, building exteriors; interior designers saw colors, fabrics, light; and the practical ones saw chairs, tables, and places to park your bum. That hasn't gone away (although some would argue it is becoming less and less important—our apologies to our commercial real estate friends), however, more important in these days of global connectivity is the virtual workplace and marketplace (for example, LinkedIn). And that is where we would like to turn your attention when thinking about how me becomes we; how does space become place in an ever more virtual world? The social medium that makes this real is your social network.

Net Worth = Network

Your net worth is driven by your network. What's the value, then, of a leader's social network, for example? In our last section, we talked about how purposeful organizations need to recruit, train, and retain leaders. Leaders come with all kinds of valuable skills, experience, education, temperament, and vision. But they also bring their social networks with them—they bring not only the me but also the we.

And that is ever more valuable today than yesterday because, in the words of John Chambers, CEO of Cisco:

"We compete against market transitions, not competitors. Product transitions used to take five or seven years: now they take one or two."

You can't sense these transitions if you are focused on your own organization and functional silos. A leader's social network is the glue that keeps him or her connected to the larger world where these transitions start and grow.

What is a Social Network?

What is a social network? It's not just your golf buddies or old college roommates. Sure, that can be part of it, but we're talking about that larger group of contacts, acquaintances and friends a leader has. And it is intentional—it's the place you live and work.

What Does a Social Network Do?

A well-managed social network brings a leader three things:

1. *Time to search for novel information:* Decreased time increases value. A well-functioning network enables a leader to find new information more quickly—it functions as an early warning system, like radar.
2. *Breadth of searchable space:* Increased space reduces uncertainty. A wider net can be cast because the effort to collect information, analyze data, and reach conclusions is spread across a group of people.
3. *Trust in the source:* History, reputation, and value (increased veracity). Over time, leaders can assess the probability that the information they are receiving from the network is true and correct.

It makes your community that much stronger, that much larger, and when focused on shared purpose, that much more effective in living out a leader's purpose.

How Do You Make It Work?

There are four major tactics you can use to effectively manage your social network. Great leaders do these things consciously, consistently, and conscientiously:

1. *Align with your personal purpose.* First and foremost, if your social network is not supporting you in living out your purpose, it is of marginal use. It needs to be pulling you into the future—sometimes kicking and screaming.

2. *Actively manage.* This requires effort; it means setting aside time to contact people and doing it on a regular basis. A good rule of thumb is having deliberate contact monthly, ideally with face-to-face meetings several times a year.

3. *Seek diversity.* Members of the network should bring different subject matter expertise, predispositions (i.e., caution vs. risk taking), and demographic perspectives to you. And there should always be at least one naysayer in the network who can be counted on as a brake or a Devil's Advocate.

4. *Effective leaders' social networks are not static.* They need to change over time as leaders mature and evolve themselves. Members will need to be swapped out and replaced for any number of reasons. The biggest reason is you don't want your network turning into group think.

Summing Up

Space and place are connected through brand. Brand is about the visible shared purpose you have within your community. And it gets lived out, in today's world, through your social network. Place is not by accident; it can be consciously constructed and maintained. So can your social network.

Now, we turn to the practice of shared purpose through leverage. This section has been about the where and who of purpose and the New Story of Work; now we will tackle the intersection of Purpose and Practice—how and what.

"Earning is surviving. Learning is thriving."

PART III – PRACTICE AND WORK

Chapter 13: **Leveraging Shared Purpose**

So, where are we in our story about putting Shared Purpose to work? Let's do a brief review. This entire discussion started with the realization that most of our social institutions are either failing or have become dysfunctional—they no longer promote the well-being of people and their communities.

Given that premise, we have begun to lay out a process that can provide the vision of a different context for the social contract that people typically have with their governing institutions. First, the New Story, or the new context of work, centers on people having, knowing, and understanding their purpose. Second, that purpose is anchored in physical and other types of community, which gives them a sense of place. Now, we get to the So what?

Make It Happen: Talk the Talk and Walk the Walk

How can people leverage purpose and place so that they impact the largest possible collection of humanity? That brings us to this section about practice in the sense of: What do you do every day, day in and day out, to consciously live out a personal and shared purpose?

Well, it depends. It depends on what role you have assumed in your organization or community. For simplicity's sake, we have divided those roles into three groups: leaders, managers, and a new group we call creative catalysts. What we would like to suggest is that the form of practice each group engages in will be somewhat, even radically, different than others. The key is realizing which group you fall into. Let's take them one at a time.

"A genuine leader is not a searcher for consensus but a molder of consensus." ~ Martin Luther King, Jr.

Leaders

A leader's practice centers on creating and exploring. As we said in the last section, leaders focus on doing the right thing. That's where their leverage is located. *Doing the right thing for the largest group of people possible magnifies their impact.*

The secret to a leader's practice is determining just what is the right thing. Leaders find themselves at the center of attention for many competing interests. Who is right? Who is only out for their own advantage? How does all this get sorted out? Going back to our first idea that all action needs to come from intentional purpose, perhaps a way to do this is to test the competing concerns.

Is this about monetary profits, or is it about the welfare of others? We've mentioned it before, that if purpose towards serving a greater good comes first, the profit or its equivalent will often follow. Once key questions have been asked and answered, a leader can articulate core values, point the community in a new direction, and reinforce cultural norms, which spread the wealth, so to speak. As the head moves, the body follows. Leaders know the importance of being a story leader, sharing value, being social, and walking their talk.

Managers

A manager's practice focuses on setting or maintaining a new normal for the community. Their practice is about getting to where the leader points. The way they leverage that is by starting new initiatives towards the shared purpose. And the unique way they do this is through judicious stewardship of resources. For example, they can use an allocation-of-energy matrix to map their actions:

Allocation of Energy Matrix

Managers constantly scan their activities to see what they need to stop doing, slow down, maintain a status quo, speed up, and start anew. The logic to this practice is finding energy and resources in things that have stopped and slowed, which can be re-allocated to other things that need new beginnings or more attention.

Creative Catalysts

It's difficult to describe how creative catalysts leverage their practice. These are the people who Richard Florida described as the "super creatives." About twelve percent of the population's focal point is to find problems not yet realized. Creative catalysts are often seen as somewhat strange and even eccentric.

They do their own thing, don't follow rules very well, and are highly intuitive. These are the folks who are the boundary spanners in communities. They bridge different ways to practice. In a sense they create expansive narratives that integrate ideas from many different perspectives. Often they appear to generate ideas and practices out of thin air.

Creative catalysts cannot be managed in a traditional sense. But they can be encouraged to look in new and different directions. "Hey, why don't you go look at <this new thing>?" There are two basic strategies to leverage this directed action into shared purpose. One technique is to give creative catalysts tools of expression so they can communicate with larger and larger groups. In today's world, this amounts to wide ranging access to social media, complemented with more traditional means such as writing, expressive art, and video.

The second way to leverage creative catalysts is to pair them with others who have different subject matter expertise. You get things like astro-biologists, theater engineers, and perhaps spiritual healers. It is most curious that this group has the highest potential to leverage shared purpose simply because they operate in the unknown regions of human endeavor. These are the people who pull the future into the present—they are literally working the future, today.

Creative Catalysts are Literally Working the Future! Today

Creative catalysts offer hope of a new, better tomorrow in today's world, where we operate day-to-day on reptilian emotions and monkey motives, we are governed by medieval institutions, and we worship at the altar of technology. Leave them out and you could die a slow death.

The Challenge
So, who are you: leader, manager, or catalyst? We have one closing question for you. If you are operating out of your realized purpose, and you are standing in a place of shared community, what are you going to do tomorrow to leverage your abilities to promote well-being by a factor of ten, or even more?

When you have an answer to that question, you will have your own purpose pathway laid out for all to see and follow.

Now, we have opened the door to a New Story of Work; we've talked about the True North Star of Shared Purpose; given you a map of the new place territory; and offered some ideas of how to practice this within each of our major role categories.

The next section brings us full circle, and with the focus on the creative catalyst role, talks about how brand transformation can lead the way.

PART III – PRACTICE AND WORK

Chapter 14: **The Purpose of Transformation**

This section is a summary of sections on our need for a New Story of Purpose and:

> • **Purpose = Leadership**;
> • **Place = Linkage**; and
> • **Practice = Leverage**.

To pull all this together with a clear view of the path forward, we have some thoughts on those perennially popular corporate topics: *collaboration, innovation,* and *transformation*.

The Old Story of Profit First is dying, and there is nothing to replace it. What we desperately need and yearn for is a New Story of Purpose First. Companies must become prophets of the new, so they can continue to earn new profits. In order for companies to accumulate wealth, they must not only share the wealth but also ultimately recognize the role of all parties in the co-creation of that wealth.

Transformation Nation

Sadly, so many people have neither work nor a life, which is made dramatically evident by the rapid rise in our suicide rates and lack of civic engagement across almost all demographics—the United States of Alienation.

Collaboration

People do not truly collaborate unless they know their best interests have been fully embraced. That is called shared purpose. Innovation does not happen in a vacuum—it is part of an interconnected chain of simultaneous events, factors, and influences such as shared purpose, vision, leadership, inspiration, imagination, and invention; all that which leads to shared value creation.

What combines shared purpose and co-creation of a future desired state is community, and from both the corporate and stakeholder points of view the ultimate fruit of these unions is called commonwealth, wealth for all, not just for the One Percent. Within the corporation that commonwealth is called culture—all that you do and don't do relative to others in the minds, hearts, and wallets of your brand community of stakeholders and beyond.

You cannot tell a good story unless you have a good story. A good story is simultaneously personal and universal. There is no point in creating a New Story unless it has value for all concerned and affected. It cannot have value unless it is built on shared values.

154

The Purpose-Profit Connection

In the New Story (and in the new world of work), there is a direct connection between purpose and profit. All healthy businesses are founded with a core purpose and values, as well as a vision, mission, and value proposition. Purpose has to come before profit, not only at the inception of a business, but all through the business lifecycle. Increasingly the more stakeholders have an ever-renewing brand, a new sense of positive purpose and value, the more profitable and sustainable a business will be. Customer experience and content are made from these threads.

Transformation is not a standalone concept. It is like a valued brand: An active, shared, positive, and aligned purposeful culture, which is built on a foundation of strong emotional transformative experiences such as a sustaining story of origin—why we exist and whom we serve. A healthy, vibrant sustainable culture has three legs:

Cultural Sustainability

Visionary Leadership   **Empathetic Management**   **Creative Catalysts**

Each leg is supported by its brand community of stakeholders. The stronger the community, the stronger and smoother support for the three legs of the culture. Incremental innovation is possible without a purposeful culture. However, continual transformation is only possible in a purposeful culture, and without continual transformation businesses will not be sustainable. They will be tomorrow's corporate road kill, killed by relentless competition, change, and transformation.

Work The Future, Today: *Collaboration, Innovation, Transformation*
There are two basic processes that bring the future to you and your organization: innovation and transformation. Too much has been written about innovation and too precious little on transformation. And neither is truly possible without collaboration, which is often misunderstood.

Collaboration, at a conceptual level, involves:

- **Awareness:** We become part of a working entity with a shared purpose.
- **Motivation:** We drive to gain consensus in problem-solving or development.
- **Self-synchronization:** We decide as individuals when things need to happen.
- **Participation:** We participate in collaboration and we expect others to participate.
- **Mediation:** We negotiate, collaborate, and find a middle point.
- **Reciprocity:** We share and we expect sharing in return through reciprocity.

- **Reflection:** We think and consider alternatives.
- **Engagement:** We proactively engage rather than wait and see.

Innovation is the harnessing of creative thought to a useful end for a short-term goal.

Transformation is:

- Future value creation for a shared long-term goal.
- A shared act of imagination translated into a treasured future.
- The art of scientifically bringing creativity continuously to life.
- Applied creativity that makes a long-term difference.
- Irreversible, substantive, creates new identity, and contains a shift in purpose.
- A shared activity where people come together to co-create the future today and create something of lasting value.

Transformation is ultimately about the collective quest for meaning at work, play, and life—to be better together.

It might be said that true and sustainable transformation is about creating an ever-renewing story encapsulated in a living breathing brand/culture. The three ingredients of a sustainable culture in the new world of work are:

1. **Brand Purpose** (WHY: passion, promise, and perception)
2. **Brand Participation** (WHO + HOW: partnership, participation, and process)
3. **Brand Performance** (WHAT + WHEN + WHERE: planet, people, and profits)

So, What's *Your* New Story?

Purpose, leadership, and place let you pull the future towards you. You surround it, you dance with it, you make it real and share it with others.

The outlines of the New Story narrative are emerging from the fog of the past. It's more than about harmony instead of control; it's more feminine than masculine; it's more about stewardship than exploitation; it's more about co-creation than about what's already built. And it's more about living in the present with an eye to the future than not being present and looking toward the past.

We conclude our manifesto with a playbook to get you started on your pathway to *purpose, possibility,* and *plenty*. The path to sustainable profits is through shared, aligned positive purpose.

REVOLUTION

PART III – PRACTICE AND WORK

Chapter 15: **The Way of the Path to Purposeful Transformation**

"The cave you fear to enter holds the treasure that you seek."
~ Joseph Campbell

Finding Your True North

The way to make the emotional transformation towards purpose parallels the classic story of the Hero's Journey. It is a path of what Carl Jung called individualization or becoming oneself. Or, in an organizational setting, finding your purpose—your True North. The process by which this occurs is called differentiation and has as a goal of the development of the individual or organizational personality, the discovery and acceptance of one's true purpose. So, back to the Purpose Path. It is often summarized as having seven distinct, but overlapping, stages.

The Brand New Path to Purpose

We started this section talking about new, emerging realities in the world of work. We looked at why some of us may be stuck in the Old Story and World, and considered some key questions about who we are. Then we spent some time looking in some detail at three different ways of looking at ourselves.

Now, we are at a point in our journey where we need to look at just how we're supposed to be able to make this transition to purposeful and sustainable transformation. Use this seven-step path to guide you and your organization through this transition. The table below outlines the steps in the order you'll take them. For each step, you'll see the name of the state associated with that step, the *quality* you should be experiencing during that particular stage of transition and the *activity* you'll associate with that step:

7 Steps: THE PURPOSE PATH

0. Brand Step (#) **/ Brand Stage of the Purpose Path** (State)

• **Brand Action** (Quality)

• **Brand Focus**

• **Brand Development** (Activity)

FORMAT

1. Initiation: Recognizing the Real World

• *Socialization:* Looking from outside to inside.

• Your focus is on your BRAND.

• Awareness that something is missing and time is passing. You move to get something you need. You begin seeking answers to nagging questions, such as "What is our core purpose?"

2. Involvement: Call to Adventure

• *Struggle:* Looking from inside to outside.

• Your focus is your BRAND IN THE MARKETPLACE.

• Looking at parts of ourselves we don't want to look at. Introspection: "Is it us or has the world changed without us?"

3. Inquiry: **Meeting the Mentor** (hire us!)

• *Service:* Moving from inside to outside.

• Your focus is on your BRAND COMMUNITY.

• Sharing what we know in order to build future capability with our stakeholders and the communities we do business in. Sharing provides a bridge from what was to the New Story.

4. Improvement: **Crossing the Threshold**

• *Showtime:* Going from old playbook to new.

• Your focus is on BRAND ACTIVATION.

• Creativity is expressed through innovative culture. You experience the "flow" state and begin to act in brand new ways, building off the old into long-term sustainability.

5. Inspiration: **Road of Trials**

• *Sensing:* Opening up to co-creation.

• Your focus is on COLLABORATION WITH BRAND COMMUNITY.

• Actively co-creating brand value and perception. Firmly committed to a pathway of purposeful change.

6. Innovation: **Seizing the Prize**
- *Stewardship*: Walking your talk.
- Your focus is on BRAND LEADERSHIP.
- Realizing and acting upon new marketplace demands such as authenticity, transparency, responsibility, and engagement.

7. Iteration: **Return with the Treasure**
- *Simplification*: Knowing shift happens.
- Your focus is on your BRAND FUTURE.
- Oh, shift! Developing a firm grasp of the obvious: Purpose = Profits. Change, complexity, and competition are relentless and ruthless.

Call to Action *for a Brand New World*
Humans change at the speed of snails but everything around us changes quickly and all the time, with ever greater velocity, impact, and complexity. We all need a flexible new framework. We call this *contextual reimagination*. If you want to grow or keep growing your brand, you need to keep it new and stay focused on your shared purpose and value. If you want to find out how it is done or want us to do it with you, contact us through **www.workthefuture.today**.

"From Me to We to US. And from He to She to We to US"

Purpose
1

Place
2

Practice
3

CONCLUSION

Chapter 16: **Working The Future, Together**

We have come to the end of this journey. Time to pull all the loose threads of our existence together and weave a tapestry of working the future, together and now. This is our message of hope and help for humanity.

There is no today, the here and now, without yesterday and tomorrow. There is no now, without before and later. They're all relative to one another and we're all similarly related… in relationship to one another and the planet we share—our only planet—of which we are an inseparable part. So, here's how we work the future, today, to build a better future together.

Know Now, or Now How

We work the future today, as tomorrow might never come if we don't do what we need to do today. As we all share a common destiny, we are all in it together, so we might as well be better together. To be better together we must share a better future together—united we stand, divided we fall today and tomorrow.

To enjoy a better future together, we must start working together, today, to co-create a better future together. As the future is a series of todays, of new nows, we must co-create that new, better now by asking: How can we start, now? And since we share an inescapable web of mutuality, we need to work together to create a better future together.

Innovate Today, Transform Tomorrow

Innovation is about a better today, whereas transformation is about a better tomorrow, so we must innovate but we must, more importantly, transform the past, today, and tomorrow into a better future for all of us by collaborating and co-creating shared and aligned purpose and value to create a future that we will value today, tomorrow, and long into the future.

The Heart of the Matter

So, we must always ask ourselves: What are we right now? What is it that we wish to become next, soon, later, much later, and long into the future? It is this transitional state that is the heart of the matter. As we all know, the future matters because if we don't act intentionally then the future will happen but probably not in the way we want it to.

Embrace Your Future

We have the power to shape the future while dancing with uncertainty, ambiguity, and constant change, along with embracing the chaos, confusion, and complexity that come with it. We need to know what our being is based on—which purpose and values—and then, having a clear idea of what our gift to the world is, share it.

Hope in a Hopeless World

"When we are no longer able to change a situation, we are challenged to change ourselves." ~ Viktor E. Frankl, *Man's Search for Meaning*

We are not only human beings, but we are also human becomings. We are in a permanent state of becoming something new—in a transitional state of turning this into that. We are co-creating the future, today, which makes us human creatings as well.

You Can't Take It with You

There are many in our global consumer culture who believe that having is the ultimate expression of their humanity. In truth, the only thing we have is a mirage of owning something, and that, like everything else, is only with us until death or the onset of senility at best.

In his book, *Man's Search For Meaning*, Viktor Frankl said that no matter what, when we have nothing else, we always have a choice in how we respond to life. How will we act? Not react, but act. The power to decide how we respond to life—no matter what it might throw at us—and to land on our feet, is ours.

Charles Eisenstein asks about the future: How do we make a better, more beautiful world inside and outside of ourselves and amongst ourselves and beyond? What is the key to life? The key to life is knowing that life is what you make it. What we make it. What we make it together collectively, today and tomorrow, building on the past.

From the Personal to the Universal

If we care for ourselves, we must care for others. If we care for others, then we must share. Sharing is daring to care by giving. It's not stuff but life itself that gives us relatedness, interbeing, being part of something much greater than ourselves, and being part of this life system called earth.

So we need to work together, to come together, to be together, to enjoy a better future together. How do we do this? We do this starting today in the here and now, not the over there and later. We work the future, today, as the future starts now, not later, and time waits for no one.

To Work The Future! Today, follow the steps in each of these three categories:

1. **Purpose**
2. **Place**
3. **Practice**

Purpose provides the pathway to a better future for oneself and others. Place provides the pathway to a place and space where others who matter to us—and to whom we matter—congregate. Practice is the pathway to the means by which we bring purpose to life in community with others.

- *Purpose* **is the great why of life.**

- *Place* **is the great home of the why, who, and where of life.**

- *Practice* **is the great how and what of life.**

When you combine purpose, place, and practice into the pathway to greater individual and shared possibilities, you get a powerful combination of infinite complexity, richness, and power.

So how to make a better world, not a world filled with more or better stuff? We know that a new better world is built on beauty, bounty, and being better together through a pathway: a plan, a place, a practice, to bring all our gifts to life, to share them with one another and to combine them into a future worth enjoying together. We have many, many known and unknown masterpieces in this world.

The music of Mozart, the paintings of van Gogh, the sculptures of Rodin, the writings of Shakespeare, and so many other masterpieces make our ordinary lives special. Our lives are filled with wonders, treasures, mysteries, and miracles of imagination and creativity. We are surrounded every day by the many gifts of others who collectively over the years have made the world what it is today. Everything is built on the efforts of those who came before us.

We have much to thank from the Old Story of Profit First. The profit motive has driven tremendous change through exploration, experimentation, invention, discovery, and design. In the search for new profits, new markets, and new monopolies, capitalism and market forces invited the development and expression of much human ingenuity, inventiveness, and creativity. This led to a substantial rise in the living standards of many people on this planet. Much good and much bad has come of this. We need to celebrate, appreciate, and enjoy the many benefits that have been derived from this seemingly endless capitalist expression through expansion, exploitation, and consumption. But enough is more than enough.

In summary, we need to embrace that which is good, helpful, and beneficial, and to reject the more damaging, negative, and inhumane aspects of global capitalism and the greed, power-seeking, and craving that never seem to end.

To be better together, we must make it long term. To make it long term, we need to ask how to be better together today, tomorrow, and the day after. And it's not just asking: Why? but also asking Why not? Why and why not are followed by who and where, which are then followed by what, how, and when.

The Future Is Now

So, no more mañanas. What we need more of is asking: What to do today? What do we need, what must, should, could we do today to have a better life tomorrow? What works is working the future, today, doing what we can, what we must do today, to have a better future together, tomorrow. We are human becomings. We, like time, like the world, like life, are always in transition from one state to another—transitioning from this into that.

• What kind of world do you want to co-create for yourself, your children, grandchildren, and the generations to come?

• Are you going to be a proactive participant or a passive passenger along the pathway of life? Stop doing so much and start creating more!

• Our brand-new purpose in the 21st century is: In good we trust. In gold we rust. Money can buy comfort, but it can't buy happiness.

"I'm very optimistic about the future. I'm not optimistic because I think our problems are small, I'm optimistic because I think our capacity to deal with problems is great." ~ Danny Hillis, The Long Now Foundation

The future is far too important to wait until tomorrow—we must Work The Future! Today

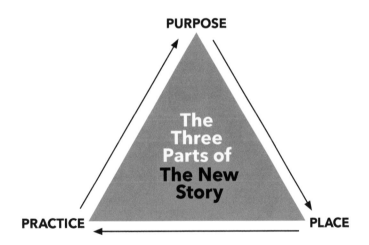

PURPOSE

The Three Parts of The New Story

PRACTICE

PLACE

173

"The future ain't what it used to be."

CHAPTER SUMMARIES

PART 1: PURPOSE

We start with talking about purpose because that is the fundamental guiding principle in the transition from the Old Story Of Profit First to the New Story of Purpose First. Purpose is the grounding, the point at which everyone connects in the transition. There's been much said lately about purpose. Many opinions, many definitions. We don't want to any chance of misunderstanding, so we explain what purpose is to us and why we believe it is absolutely bedrock to all that follows. As every good pilot knows, you check your compass reading and your altitude indicator before you take off. If you don't, you'll never really know where you are on the journey. Following that best practice, we start with a check on our compass—purpose and direction.

Chapter 1: **This into That**

Why even read this book? Because the world has lost its way. We have no clear core purpose, thanks to our misleaders and misleading institutions. We need a new illuminating North Star to guide our journey—the New Story of Purpose, of being better together.

Chapter 2: **What's Your Why, and Why's That?**

We share a summary of the highlights from our research that asked thoughtful people about their "Why?" and "Why's that?" What we found was that the "why of life" is about experience, being present in this world, not just doing or having something. Also, we found that finding a place to work on purpose–a place where people could live out their why–was a difficult idea to wrap their heads around.

Chapter 3: **So, What's Your Story?**

The first part of your story is your purpose. The middle part of your story is about the values you hold sacred and how you know when you are living out those values. The last part is about how you bring the New Story into being. We look at how your purpose and story are perceived, what people see you doing in the act of sharing, and what you are in fact sharing.

Chapter 4: **Do You Live in the Right Place?**

We conclude the discussion of purpose by shifting the focus to examine where purpose and your value story get lived out–putting purpose in its place within your life. People often get confused about the words "space" and "place." We define and discuss those in this chapter. Lessons of this chapter apply equally to your home, your workplace, and your community. This chapter sets the stage for the next section.

PART 2: PLACE

Having a clear purpose is all well and good, but where does it get played out in time and space? That question is about what we call "place." The place we are all most familiar with is the community we live in, the neighborhood where our house or apartment is located. Just as the forces of change from the old to the new are creating change for individuals, so they are driving change in our communities. If change is scary for people, it is downright terrifying for our towns and cities government. Spaces of old become places for tomorrow.

Chapter 5: Will Your Community be 'Dead On Arrival' in the 21st Century?

Just like people without purpose, communities without a purpose and an identity to live out will not make the transformation to the New Story. This chapter addresses what you can do to integrate your purpose with that of your community.

Chapter 6: How to Keep the DOA from Happening to Your Community

We received much positive feedback on our original op-ed about the major challenges facing local governments in the early 21st century. Folks asked us to expand on how to keep these oncoming forces of change at bay. This chapter shows how you can make these forces work for you—not against you—if you have a strategy.

Chapter 7: **So, What's Your Community Brand?**

As we discussed in chapter 3, everybody needs a purpose-anchored story. So do communities, if they are to help you live out your personal purpose. A brand is how you frame that story—it is a living, breathing, ever-changing relationship. Your civic brand is a clearly defined and identified entity with an associated promise of value and purpose.

Chapter 8: **How to Move Your Community Forward**

This chapter offers specific tactics for moving your community forward, based on a model of a purposeful place brand:

1. *Strategy*: Putting someone in charge of strategic planning, branding, and innovation.
2. *Services*: Developing a plan for consolidation of services as revenues collapse.
3. *Sustainability*: Making continuous sustainability your central policy goal.

Chapter 9: **Putting Your Place Brand on the Map**

Branding your place is important because your town is in competition with hundreds, if not thousands, of other local governments for highly talented and resourceful residents, businesses, and organizations. You want the economic engine of the 21st century—"that creative class of people" as Richard Florida has called them—to come live, stay, and grow their families and businesses in your town. Branding is the emotional magnet that will draw them to you, and keep them there.

Practice

PART 3: PRACTICE AND WORK

If you have followed us so far, you understand about purpose-driven change, and you can see how place can support that transformation. OK, so what? How do you accomplish this? First we describe the structure of our New Story of Work; next, we focus on the purpose of leadership; finally, we look at the purpose of place and the purpose of practice. We close out our story stressing the need for big picture thinking, co-creation, and shared purpose. Finally, we lay out a step-by-step method for making the emotional and organizational transformation required to move from the Old Story to the New Story of Work.

Chapter 10: **Reimagining the Context of Work–Why Purpose?**

This brings us full circle to purpose in the context of work, where many of us find our highest purpose. However, we live in an increasingly purposeless world filled with purposeless work. The Old Story and its attendant social institutions were designed to promote continuous growth. These institutions are no longer life affirming, nor supportive of personal well-being (integration of body, mind, and spirit), let alone human wholeness (integration of individuals into a greater whole). This chapter introduces the key next steps to bring purpose more fully into work.

Chapter 11: **Leading with Purpose**

Leaders show their followers a direction to move towards. They lead them towards something, and that something is purpose. In an ideal case the leader, followers, and organization are all aligned on a commonly understood and embraced purpose. This chapter explores how that gets done.

Chapter 12: **Place Linkage—Where Purpose Gets Connected**

In our last chapter, we talked about how leaders express purpose, how managers make it real, and how creative catalysts actually create purpose. We switch gears a bit in this chapter to focus on how that purpose, and ultimately shared purpose, gets expressed in physical and virtual environments. If the previous chapter could be called the what, this one is the where.

Chapter 13: **Leveraging Shared Purpose**

How can people leverage purpose and place so that they impact the largest number of people? That question brings us to this chapter about practice—what do you do every day, day in and day out, to consciously live out a personal and shared purpose. We explore the role you assume in your work organization or community. We look at leaders, managers, and creative catalysts.

Chapter 14: The Purpose of Transformation
The Old Story of Profit First is dying, and there is nothing to replace it. We yearn for a New Story of Purpose First to take the place of the burnt out husk of the Old. We need to bring that story to life and to put it to work for all stakeholders, not just shareholders. Companies must not only share the wealth their workers create, but recognize the role of all parties in the co-creation of that wealth.

Chapter 15: The Way of the Path Towards Purposeful Transformation
The emotional transformation towards purpose in many ways parallels the classic story of the Hero's Journey. It is a path of what Carl Jung, the noted Swiss psychiatrist who founded analytical psychology, called individualization or becoming oneself. Or, in an organizational setting, finding your core purpose means discovering your True North.

Chapter 16: A Message of Hope: Work The Future! Today
We wrap it up by reviewing where we've come in our journey to the future. So we need to work together, to come together, to be together, to enjoy a better future together. How do we do this? We do this starting today in the here and now, not the over there and later. We work the future, today, as the future starts now, not later, and time waits for no one.

"Your future starts today. So, what now?"

THE PRACTICE

Work The Future! Today is a pathfinding practice co-founded by its two managing partners, Charlie Grantham and Whitney Vosburgh.

WTF! What's The Future? What just happened? Guess what? Shift happens. And in case you didn't notice... it just happened again... on a y-u-g-e scale. Irreversibly so. We're here to Work The Future! Today with you to help you and your stakeholders move away from the old and toward the new world of both opportunity and uncertainty.

So what's your story for 2018 and beyond?

WTF! What's The Transformation? Work The Future! Today: The art of the possible practiced, well in advance. We build trust, inspire belief, and create better tomorrows—today—for forward facing clients and their communities. We work with leaders and teams to make the transition from the Old Story to the New Story. Humankind has reached a point in its evolution where it can consciously choose between creation and destruction. Our goal is to participate in the birth of the New Story. Ask yourself:

"If you knew what tomorrow would look like, what would you be doing today?"

Our purpose is to help people answer and act on this one basic question.

Acting as a trusted advisor to our clients, we provide a pathway of best practices tailored to meet people and organizations where they can make best uses of what we offer. Overall, there is a foundation to our offering that over time increases our impact and eventually the change we help co-create becomes irreversible.

Call to Action *for a Brand New World*

Humans change at the speed of snails but everything around us changes quickly and all the time, with ever greater velocity, impact, and complexity. We all need a flexible new framework. We call this *contextual reimagination*. If you want to grow or keep growing your brand, you need to keep it new and stay focused on your shared purpose and value. If you want to find out how it is done or want us to do it with you, contact us through **www.workthefuture.today,** or on Twitter at **@WorkFutureToday**, or by email at **whitneyandcharlie@workthefuture.today**.

This is Version 1 of this book,
which is the first **WTF!** book in a series
on Working The Future! Today.

Since this book is an iterative process—always
growing—please share any suggestions with us by
email (whitneyandcharlie@workthefuture.today)
that might it clearer and ever more useful, thanks!

Dr. Charles Grantham, Co-Pathfinder, has a rich multi-disciplinary background, and pursues his passion for helping leaders, organizations, and communities realize their true potential for effective performance, governance, and sustainability. After serving in the Special Forces—no, he can't tell you about it—he enjoyed successful careers in academia and with multi-national technology companies as an Executive Director of R&D. Charlie received his Ph.D. in Sociology from the University of Maryland. He has published nine books and several dozen technical papers. His last book was "ForeSight 2025," a practical guide on how to navigate the change process to prosper in the coming decade. Charlie actually worked with the original prototypes for Dilbert and the Gang… yes, all true!

Whitney Vosburgh, Co-Pathfinder, has a world of experience having lived, studied, and worked in Asia, Europe, and America. He is CEO of Brand New Purpose, a brand transformation consultancy that creates purpose-built, value-driven opportunities. Whitney is also a consulting Chief Marketing Officer and change agent for Fortune 20 companies and pivotal Silicon Valley startups. He has guided over $20 billion and counting worth of M&A, IPOs, sales, and launches. Graduated with a M.A. in Social Change from Graduate Theological Union and with a B.F.A. from Parsons School of Design. His expertise on the Future of Work has been featured in four books, including a bestseller by Dan Pink. You can find him at **@brandguru** on Twitter.

Whitney's
and Charlie's
New Book:
Work The Future!
Today 2018 Pocket
Pal: A *faster* path
to purpose, passion
and profit
WTF! (August 2018)

Charlie's Books *(books in red are for sale on Amazon):*

ForeSight 2025 (with N. Owen, T. Musch) CreateSpace: Amazon (January 2013)

Work on the Move (D. Coles ed.) International Facilities Management Association Foundation (October 2011)

Cut It Out (with Shad Arnold et. al.) International Facilities Management Association Foundation (September 2009)

Corporate Agility (James Ware and Cory Williamson) American Management Association Press (August 2007)

Consumer Evolution: 9 Effective Business Strategies for Growth (with Judy Carr) John Wiley and Sons/Gartner Press (September 2002)

Communities of Commerce (with S. Bressler) McGraw-Hill/CommerceNet Press (June 2000)

The Future of Work, McGraw-Hill/CommerceNet Press (November 1999)

Informatics, Organization and Society, Co-editor, Oldenburg Verlag (1993)

The Digital Workplace: Designing Groupware Platforms (with L.D. Nichols)

ThankYou

Charlie would like to thank:

All those who helped us, put up with our non-stop requests for comments, and were patient enough to hang in there as we created this concept and book. And obviously to all those who have given thoughtful endorsements to this earth shattering, ground breaking, utterly cosmic vision of the future. Yes, and the muse. Paying it forward thanks to those who will read our work and whose lives will be changed.

Whitney would like to thank:

Ceil Tilney for her enduring enthusiasm and excellent editing. Ben Gioia for his generous support and valuable insights. Laurie King for her skillful editing and suggestions. Leon Altman for his helpful writing tips. Elektra Vosburgh for her sharp eye and keen design advice. Heather Merriam for her love, support, and feed back. All the kind folks who answered our PurposeQuest survey and wrote testimonials—you know who you are. And finally, to all our readers.

"No planet, no people, no profits."

**Now you have the compass—
are you going to create *your* future?**

WorkTheFuture Today

Or, are you going to let the future control you?

Your choice.

CPSIA information can be obtained
at www.ICGtesting.com
Printed in the USA
BVHW021650161118
533152BV00001B/1/P

9 780999 634608